4661

G. RAYMOND

Prayer and the Christian's Devotional Life

Radiant BOOKS
Gospel Publishing House/Springfield, Mo. 65802

02-0878

©1980 by the Gospel Publishing House,
Springfield, Missouri 65802.
All rights reserved.
Library of Congress Catalog Card Number: 80-83522
ISBN 0-88243-878-6
Printed in the United States of America

A teacher's guide for individual or group study with this book
is available from the Gospel Publishing House.

Contents

1

Christ's Prayer And Devotional Life

Do we not believe that Jesus Christ is the Son of God? If so, why should Christ need times for prayer? As the Son of God was He not above such needs during His life on earth?

Because of the attacks of unbelievers on the great truths of the Word of God, believers put emphasis on the fact of Christ's deity. The Bible teaches this truth in no uncertain terms. If Jesus Christ is not God, we have no Saviour.

If God had perfect incarnation in Jesus Christ, then Jesus' life and deeds and spirit must have been a perfect revelation of God. Everything that Jesus is He is because He and the Father are one—so perfectly one that He could not misrepresent God. He is God!

Divine Yet Human

While the sacred writers proclaim the deity of Christ in the loftiest of language, they with equal vigor assert His total humanity. He was God, but He was also truly human. He has no earthly father, for He was virgin born. But He had a human mother and that made Him a human being.

The incarnation of Christ was the filling full of a human nature by Divinity. It made the man in whom

5

the miracle occurred an absolutely perfect man. It did not make Him something other than man. If it had, all His value as a Redeemer would have been made null and void.

Yes, Jesus was a real human being—spirit, soul, and body. He went through the orderly stages of growth as a child. He did not act as a man when He was a boy. He became subject to His parents and learned a trade. He worshiped in the synagogue, rejoiced at a wedding, wept at a grave. Weariness was His portion as were hunger, thirst, physical agony, and death. His emotions were real—anger over hypocrisy, groaning in the presence of unbelief, sorrowing over Jerusalem, loving as no one ever loved. Tempted in all points as we are, He was without sin.

80 Versus 30

Jesus Christ is God and the Son of God at the same time. He is also the Son of Man. In the Gospels, our Lord used the title *Son of Man* over 80 times. Paul used the term in Acts 7:56, and John sees "one like unto the Son of man" (Revelation 1:13). The term *Son of God* appears some 30 times.

As God, Christ has always existed; yet as a man, He experienced human birth. As a man, He partook of necessary food; as God, He fed 5,000 with a boy's lunch. As a man, He enjoyed a wedding in Cana; as God, He turned water into wine. As a man, in utter weariness He fell asleep in a boat. As God, He ordered the wind and the waves into total calm.

Jesus walked and talked with men in friendly and understanding fellowship. He shared their joys and sorrows. He shed tears at their losses and comforted and helped them.

Christ is our Saviour, but He is also our example. He can, however, only be an example to those who first receive Him as Saviour.

From the Scriptures we learn that Jesus lived a life of dependence upon, communion with, and submission to the Father. The Gospels are sprinkled with illustrations of Jesus at prayer.

Luke Alone

Luke gives special attention to the prayer life of our Lord. The most common verb for prayer in the New Testament is *proseuchomai*. Of the 84 occurrences of this word, 34 are in Luke's writings. There seems to be a uniqueness about his accounts. He records nine references to Jesus' prayers. Seven of these are not mentioned by the other Gospel writers.

Luke alone records that Jesus was praying when the heavens opened at His baptism (Luke 3:21, 22). In the midst of this very meaningful experience at the outset of His public ministry, He prayed. Probably Jesus had been talking with the crowd and certainly with John the Baptist, but now He was engaged in prayer. Luke does not tell us what kind of a prayer was being offered. Whether it was a prayer of worship and adoration or of thanksgiving, petition, or intercession is not revealed. This we know: He was conversing with His Father.

Luke alone tells us that, following the healing of a leper (Luke 5:12-16) with the attendant flush of popularity, Jesus "withdrew himself into the wilderness and prayed." Besieged by multitudes and taxed with an incredible work load, Jesus refused to allow "busy-

7

ness" to make Him barren in spirit. "Busyness" must be blended with inner renewal through communion with the Father.

A Mountain His Prayer Closet

Luke alone tells us that before Jesus called the Twelve, He spent the entire previous night on a mountain in prayer (Luke 6:12). Here Jesus broke away from close companions and followers to be alone with the Father. A part of the discipline of our Lord's life was to pray alone. How amazing—this Man who had all power in himself, this Man who was God and Saviour, this Man who was the omnipotent Creator, this Man who "thought it not robbery to be equal with God"—this Man felt the need to pray, and to pray alone.

Luke alone tells us that Jesus was praying alone in Caesarea Philippi when He posed two important questions: "Whom say the people that I am? . . . But whom say ye that I am?" Peter's great declaration came in answer—"The Christ of God" (Luke 9:18-20).

Luke alone tells us that Jesus took Peter, James, and John up into a mountain "to pray" (Luke 9:28) at the time of His transfiguration. This passage brings into focus one of the first New Testament cell groups — Jesus and the three disciples with whom He prayed and shared so often.

Luke alone records that as Jesus "was praying in a certain place" His disciples requested Him to teach them to pray (Luke 11:1). From the day they answered His call, the disciples had been in close fellowship with their newfound Master. His way of life, His actions, and His words had gripped and challenged them. Often they had watched Him pray. Their overwhelm-

8

ing desire to be like Him caused them to ask, "Lord, teach us to pray."

Calling at Midnight

Luke alone chronicles the prayer parables of the friend at midnight asking for bread (Luke 11: 5-8) and the shameless widow begging the unjust judge (Luke 18:1-8). Dire necessity is the driving force in both instances.

The man in Luke 11 would never have gone to his friend's house in the middle of the night to borrow bread for himself. But when a friend arrived, famished after a long journey, a deep sense of necessity made him willing to go. How often you and I have been driven to prayer because of the demanding needs of others. The awareness of their need and our inability to meet that need drives us to prayer.

Smoky Prayers

The woman in Luke 18 pressed the judge because of desperate need. Compare this to some of our prayer times—yours and mine. Do you know what I am talking about when I say, "What smoky prayers!"? Earnest petition and then a horde of wandering thoughts—what smoky faith! A glorious sense of Christ's sufficiency, then a prolonged time of complacency. And what smoky affections! A deep sense of love to God followed by a cooling of our ardor. All such is smoking flax. But when a sense of our personal need overwhelms us, we will persist in prayer.

Luke alone records the assurance of Christ's prayer for Peter when predicting that Peter would deny Him

9

(Luke 22: 31-34). The Greek word for "prayed" here is a very strong word. It is the word *deomai,* which means "to want, wish, beseech, and to supplicate." The word denotes a great conflict of energetic and overcoming prayer. Jesus did not pray that Peter might not be tested and sifted, but that his faith should not fail. Peter was coming to a crisis hour in his life, and His Master's prayer was extremely inportant to His recovery following bitter failure.

What assurance comes to us from the Saviour's intercession for us in John 17:15—"I pray not that thou shouldest take them out of the world, but that thou shouldest keep them from the evil." He prayed for Peter; He prayed for His disciples; He prays for you and me (Hebrews 7:25).

Luke alone notes the Lord's exhortation to the disciples to pray as He entered Gethsemane where He travailed in prayer (Luke 22:40).

Tell Us Why, Luke

There must be a reason for Luke's giving so much attention to the prayers of Jesus. The record he gives us of the prayer life of the Lord and His followers is understood if we link it with his approach to the history of God's provision of salvation. To Luke, these prayers were a reminder that a new era had dawned. A new chapter was now opened regarding God's dealing with man. It is prayer in the light of the end-time tug between the now and the yet-to-come; Jesus has come, the Kingdom has come; but we wait for the fulfillment of His kingdom pledge of full salvation. Between the beginning of fulfillment and the con-summation of fulfillment, Luke quotes our Lord's command to "watch and pray."

10

Prayer Opens a New Era

Let us look again at the Lucan references. The first reference is at Jesus' baptism. While He was praying, the Holy Spirit came as a dove marking the beginning of God's final step of bringing man back to himself, just as the dove in Noah's day (Genesis 8:8) marked a new beginning of an era of God's dealing with man. There is a linking significance in the account given by Luke as he places a genealogical record between the baptism of Jesus and His temptation in the wilderness. The climaxing statement of that record is: "The son of Adam, which was the son of God" (Luke 3:38). As the last Adam, Jesus did not fail when tempted of the devil in contrast to the failure of the first Adam.

Prayer Before Decision

Before Jesus chose the Twelve, He prayed. Without doubt, the human Jesus sought guidance concerning the momentous decision He was about to make. His work was more than undergirded with prayer; it was identified with prayer.

As Jesus prayed on the mountain, He was transfigured before the three of the inner circle. Luke alone tells us of the conversation Jesus had with Moses and Elijah—concerning His death and resurrection. This prophetic scene was again linked to prayer: Jesus had gone up on the mountain to pray.

The disciples' request—"Lord, teach us to pray"— must surely relate to the Kingdom. They knew from their religious background how to say prayers. They were reaching for more. And Jesus prayed, "Thy kingdom come . . . ."

Saved From Death

Do we press the point too far if we say that the

11

Lord's resurrection was in answer to His prayer? Two of the last three utterances from the cross, as recorded by Luke, are prayers. Note the record from Hebrews 5:7: "In the days of his flesh, when he had offered up prayers and supplications with strong crying and tears unto him that was able to save him from death, and was heard in that he feared."

As Luke closes his Gospel, he climaxes with prayer and praise (Luke 24:53). As he opens the record "of all that Jesus began both to do and teach" (Acts 1:1), the focal point is still prayer. Space will not permit a review of all the happenings related to prayer in the Book of Acts. Suffice it to say that prayer has a vital part in God's history of redemption and Kingdom reality.

But there is much more to be said about the prayers of Jesus. He began His earthly ministry in prayer (Luke 3:21), continued in prayer, and ended in prayer (Luke 23:34). He continues that prayer ministry to this hour (Hebrews 7:25).

Preparation, Balance, and Strength

By His example, Jesus taught us to pray at every important junction in life. He prayed much and often. He prayed short prayers in public and long prayers in private — often all night.

Jesus prayed after a busy day. Follow Him through the incredibly busy hours in His first Galilean ministry (Mark 1). Continuing into the evening, He ministered to the multitudes. All through the twilight and into the night He toiled. Rising long before daybreak, he sought out a "solitary place, and there prayed" (Mark 1:35).

In times of great success Jesus sought the balance

and poise of the Spirit through prayer (Luke 5:16; 10:21, 22). No matter how busy He was, so steeped in prayer was His spirit that He could turn aside for times of prayer.

After attack by His enemies, He spent the night in prayer (Luke 6:11, 12). His enemies, "filled with madness," tried to get rid of Him. His weapons against their threats were not carnal; He sought communion with His Father.

For Our Learning

What lessons we can learn! When days are endless with pressing duties, when success showers us with euphoria, when tests and trials would overwhelm us — we need the balance, strength, and grace available to us through prayer. Bring your plans and purposes to God's throne. Test them by praying about them. Learn from the praying Christ to pray before you plan, to take counsel before you act. If our Lord prayed before a momentous decision (Luke 6:12) and before a crisis time (Luke 9:18), how important it is for us to do so.

The deep emotions that surged in our Lord's breast were, without fail, turned into prayer. When the Pharisees asked for a sign, He "sighed deeply in his spirit" (Mark 8:12). Again when a deaf man was brought to Him, He "sighed" (Mark 7:34). We are prone to submit to our moods and mental conflicts. From Jesus' example we learn to find release through prayer.

Precepts From the Prince of Prayers

None can question the fact that the greatest examples of proper prayer practice ever demonstrated

13

were those displayed by the Lord Jesus Christ. The Bible record indicates that Jesus taught by precept and example. And this was surely true with regard to His prayer and devotional life. The example of Christ was to be the practice of His followers.

From Jesus' example we learn three great lessons. First, He showed us the necessity of prayer. As the Son of Man, so akin to us, He was never self-sufficient, but always God-dependent.

Second, Jesus' prayers were all encompassing. Study all His prayers and all He said about prayer. Ponder the prayer He taught His disciples to pray. Bow low as you meditate on His high priestly prayer of John 17. Jesus prayed for himself, for the Father's will, for His followers, and for His enemies. He touched the throne of God as He touched the depths of human degradation.

Third, Jesus' prayers teach us the true nature of prayer. It is more than asking and receiving; it is full union with God. It is more than presenting requests and waiting for answers; it is need pouring out and grace pouring in. It is not battling God's reluctance; it is working together with God's willingness. It is not attacking a closed door; it is entering an open door. It is not forcing open a closed hand; it is taking from an open hand. "Lord, teach us to pray."

2

The Model Prayer

Our Father which art in heaven,
Hallowed be thy name.
Thy kingdom come. Thy will be done
in earth, as it is in heaven.
Give us this day our daily bread.
And forgive us our debts,
as we forgive our debtors.
And lead us not into temptation,
but deliver us from evil:
For thine is the kingdom, and the power,
and the glory, for ever. Amen.

Matthew 6:9-13

Commonly this prayer is called "The Lord's Prayer." More accurately, it is the prayer the Lord taught His disciples to pray. But because of custom and for the sake of writing, we shall use the common title, "The Lord's Prayer."

An amusing, and yet tragic, story is told of the conversation between two men who were boasting about their knowledge of the Bible. The one said to the other, "Why, you don't even know the Lord's Prayer!" The second man asserted that he most surely did. The first replied, "Then let me hear you say it." So the other fellow began, "Now I lay me down to sleep. I pray the Lord my soul to keep. If I should die before I wake, I pray the Lord my soul to take." When he finished, the challenger, taken aback, responded, "Well, you sure had me fooled. I didn't think you knew it!"

The disciples, aware of Jesus' example and sensing their personal need, said, "Lord, teach us to pray," not, "Lord, teach us a prayer."

Neither Ritual nor Form

Jesus did not intend this as a ritual prayer to be merely recited in mechanical fashion. It follows His strong denunciation against vain repetition. Jesus was teaching the "way" and the "how" of petitioning the Father. Beware lest you bog down in discussion of "how" to pray and fail to pray. To do this is as tragic as reading books on how to study the Bible but failing to read the Bible itself. Such are Satan's clever tactics.

The Lord's Prayer comprehends what true prayer involves: to whom we address ourselves and how we should present our petitions. Thousands repeat this prayer daily. But do they understand it? Do they offer it from the bottom of their hearts? Do they practice what it contains? If you really pray the Lord's Prayer, you must first give yourself to God in full consecration.

The "ABC's"

This model prayer meets every conceivable situation in life. Sublime and yet simple, the prayer launched a new sense of freedom, trust, and simplicity in prayer. The prayer itself is neither an obligation nor a fetish but an example and an inspiration. What a gem of the devotional life; what a choice lesson in the holy art of prayer — the very "ABC's" of prayer.

Seven Petitions

Let us now examine and analyze this great prayer. There are seven petitions. Three relate to God and are identified by the pronoun *thy*. Note them—"Hallowed be thy name"; "Thy kingdom come"; "Thy will be done." Four petitions (some combine these as three) relate to man and are identified by the words *our* and *us*: "Give us this day our daily bread"; "Forgive us our debts"; "Lead us not into temptation"; "Deliver us from evil."

The words of the prayer cover the subjects of worship, gratitude, submission, intercession, petition, repentance, and aspiration. God's honor, reign, will, provision, forgiveness, guidance, deliverance, and protection are sought.

Overriding Concerns

The glory of God's name, the coming of God's kingdom, the doing of God's will—these are the overriding concerns of true prayer. The finest, the greatest, and the highest aspirations of man are implied in God's glory, God's kingdom, and God's will. They comprehend all other desires and requests in prayer. The more our prayers adhere to these concerns, the greater they will be. God's name, His kingdom, and His will must precede my petition.

Prayer that pleases God is based on a right relationship. We come as children recognizing Him as our Father. We come as worshipers recognizing His name as holy and to be held in reverence. We come as His subjects submitting to Him as our King and acknowledging His authority, power, and rule. We come as servants ready to do His will on earth as it is done in heaven.

If we follow this approach to God, we lay aside our own ambitions and plans. Our approach is God-centered. We are not coming with our needs alone. We are concerned with His concerns as well as our own. His name, His honor, and His will become important to us. Above all, we do not come with blank minds and meaningless words. Coming in this manner, our concerns, His concerns, and the concerns of His people will come into beautiful focus.

Relationship

The model prayer begins with a relationship— "Our Father." Access to God is not on the basis that He is the Creator and we are His creatures. The atoning death of Christ gives us access. Our appropriation by faith makes us children of God. We are "accepted in the beloved"—none other than Christ himself (Ephesians 1:6). Our relationship to God in Christ gives us the right of a son to speak to the Father. All that a father ought to be to his children, God is to us and more.

As our Heavenly Father, God has pledged himself to provide for our needs. As His children, we are encouraged to bring our needs to Him. Jesus said:

> If ye then, being evil, know how to give good gifts unto your children; how much more shall your heavenly Father give the Holy Spirit to them that ask him? (Luke 11:13).

Immediate Access

What a privilege! Access to a loving father by a

trusting child is immediate and unquestioned. No door bars the way. No sacrifice, ablutions, or intermediary form ritualistic barriers. As our Father, God is near, His ear is open, and His heart reaches out. He is eager to receive us.

A little child was seen pounding on a door, crying, "Open, open." The knob turned, but a voice was heard from inside, "Say 'please' first." But the child cried the more frantically, "Open the door." Again from inside, "What do you say?" There was no answer, only the crying of the child. The person inside had not seen that a dog had chased the child and had bitten the child before the door was opened.

Aren't you glad that we don't have to come to God with a stereotyped "please"? If the child had said, "Please," the terror could have been relieved and the wound avoided. While there is a proper way to approach God in prayer, He is always available to our cry of distress. You don't need to use a password to get His attention.

Hallowed Be Thy Name

The word *hallow* means to pronounce or render holy. God's name is essentially holy. The meaning of the prayer is that the name of God shall be venerated, reverenced, and esteemed as holy. The thought is that God's name is to be treated as something special, above the ordinary.

We come as worshipers recognizing the sum of the attributes of God in His nature and being, as manifested in His holy name. The Psalmist has several expressions worthy of our prayerful consideration:

Because he knows and understands My name (Psalm 91:14, *Amplified*).

19

O Lord our Lord, how excellent is thy name in all the earth! (Psalm 8:1; also verse 9).

I will praise the name of God with a song, and will magnify him with thanksgiving (Psalm 69:30).

That men may know that thou, whose name alone is Jehovah, art the Most High over all the earth (Psalm 83:18).

This expression is literally a petition and really a command, "Cause your name to be hallowed." But it also focuses our thoughts in worship. We are exhorted to enter into God's presence with thanksgiving and into His courts with praise.

God's Kingdom

The second petition, "Thy kingdom come," voices the earnest request that God's sovereign rule shall come to fulfillment. The prayer expresses a yearning that people increasingly shall acknowledge the rule of Christ by self-surrender to Him and faithful obedience to Him.

From our Lord's conversation with the learned Nicodemus we find that the Kingdom, in its real and truest sense, can only come when it comes in spiritual power in the personal lives of individuals. Jesus never even permitted Nicodemus to ask a question. And the question, no doubt, would have been the one common to all Jews: "When will the kingdom be set up? When will Roman bondage cease?" Quickly Jesus broke in with, "Except a man be born again, he cannot see the kingdom of God" (John 3:3).

In our prayer life things that relate to the kingdom of God should take first place. These are things that matter most to consecrated believers. Jesus said:

"Seek ye first the kingdom of God, and his righteousness; and all these things shall be added unto you" (Matthew 6:33).

The question we must ask ourselves is: Does Christ have complete rule in our lives? Are there areas that are alien to Him? little closets where we retain selfish things? unsurrendered territory? How can we pray for His kingdom to come if we bar Him from total rule in our life, our home, our work, our pleasure?

God's Will

In keeping with our desire that God be first in all things, we pray that His will may be done in earth as it is in heaven. How is God's will done in heaven? I believe it is done willingly, joyfully, and immediately.

A mother had three sons. She asked one of them to do an errand for her. He replied, "Now, Mother? Can't you wait until I finish the game?" and he turned her down.

She went to the second one and he said, "Sure, Mom," and then promptly forgot about it in the excitement of what he was doing.

She went to the third boy who promptly dropped what he was doing and ran the errand.

"He that doeth the will of God abideth for ever" (1 John 2:17). Not he that thinks about it or talks about it, but he that does the will of God.

Daily Bread

Now the prayer shifts from petitions of aspiration for God's purposes to matters of practical and personal concern. The "daily bread" represents all those things needed to sustain physical life. Jesus is concerned with the mundane details of our lives.

The personal pronouns *I*, *my*, and *mine* are not found in the prayer. A "give-me" attitude is prompted by selfish ambition and only inflates pride and pampers carnal desires.

Jesus said, " . . . daily bread." He knew the importance of today. He did not ask for bread for tomorrow or next month. Today is the important time. The prayer is for immediate need.

Forgiving

The fifth petition also relates to personal need: "And forgive us our debts, as we forgive our debtors." The context refers to moral debts, those which sinners commit when God's moral law is violated.

The Amplified Bible states: "Forgive us our sins, for we ourselves also forgive every one who has offended us or done us wrong" (Luke 11:4).

Sin separates us from God. To harbor an unforgiving spirit is sinful. In the prayer Jesus points out there is no forgiveness for the believer who has an unforgiving spirit.

The true Christian community is a reconciled and reconciling community. The absence of love and the prevalence of criticism and strife among believers hinders answered prayer. We cannot expect continued cleansing and forgiveness if we harbor resentment, grudges, malice, and bitterness. The forgiving heart receives God's forgiveness.

True forgiveness includes never again referring to an offense once forgiven. Hard? God never remembers our sins when they have been forgiven.

Temptation

"Lead us not into temptation." Temptation is a

universal experience. Some temptations are born of our own willfulness. God never tempts us to evil (James 1:13,14), but He does permit tests and trials to come our way.

Some people live with a reckless security. The model prayer teaches us never to be presumptuous. Jesus refused to be misled even when Scripture was quoted (Luke 4:9-11). Do not presume upon God's care. God's grace and mercy are not license to sin.

Deliverance

"Deliver us from evil." This is a prayer for deliverance from evil, and it can possibly mean from the evil one. We need deliverance from both the evil one and from evil in general—evil within, evil experiences, evil companions.

Often we fail because we live too close to temptation. A little boy was in the pantry when his mother called, "Son, where are you?" He said, "In the pantry." She asked, "What are you doing?" And he replied, "I'm fighting temptation."

Jude instructs us to keep ourselves in the love of God (Jude 21). We are kept when we stay on keeping ground.

The model prayer begins with God's Person and moves to God's program. It proceeds to the needs of individuals, dealing with spiritual needs primarily. The prayer closes with a doxology ascribing praise to God.

3

What Is Prayer?

Prayer is the greatest privilege of the Christian. Through prayer my life, my service, and my very being are put in touch with the omnipotent God.

Prayer is more than an act; it is an attitude. When prayer is lowered to the level of speech, it becomes a farce. Lifted to the high level of communication with God, it becomes a force.

Prayer is the conversation of the soul with God. By it I express my appreciation for the past, my apprehension of the present, and my aspiration for the future. Prayer is the chalice of blessing and the channel of power.

True prayer takes hold of God's strength and witnesses His power in action. The true purpose of prayer is to enable us to see the supernatural power of the Almighty working to overcome the problems of life. Thus prayer becomes a weapon, a powerful weapon, for our use.

Prayer is the spreading out of my helplessness in the name of our Lord Jesus Christ before the eyes of a loving Heavenly Father. He knows and understands and cares.

Prayer is the panting of my spirit after God. It is taking hold of the willingness of God, rather than an overcoming of His reluctance.

24

Dynamite . . . Tranquility

Prayer is spiritual dynamite! It produces divine leverage. By prayer my need is connected with the supernatural storehouse.

Prayer is the road to tranquility and strength of the soul. Prayer leaves me with self-control, poise, and calmness of mind and spirit in the most trying time. "I have been driven many times to my knees," said Abraham Lincoln, "by the overwhelming conviction that I had nowhere else to go. My own wisdom, and that of all about me, seemed insufficient for the day."

Prayer is the greatest force in the world. It releases the resources of the Almighty which are beyond measure. God's promise is true—"Call unto me, and I will . . . show thee great and mighty things, which thou knowest not" (Jeremiah 33:3).

How amazing and awesome to realize that in a very real sense God has limited himself in the performing of great and mighty things to the prayers — the "calling"—of His people.

Prayer is not only my highest privilege and my most treasured joy, it can also be my most effective weapon to achieve. My ability to achieve is multiplied beyond measure by the unleashing of God's power as I look to Him in believing prayer.

Begins in Heaven

Prayer begins in heaven. I do not know what to pray for as I ought, but the Spirit makes intercession for me. Prayer becomes a mighty force through which God fulfills His purpose.

Prayer is the key of the day, the lock of the night, a shield to the soul, a sacrifice to God, and a scourge to Satan.

25

Prayer is a way of life. It is a fervent mind settled on God, a voice of faith, and a virtue that prevails against sin and Satan.

Prayer is communication with God, and the soul craves for reality in that experience. "Oh that I knew where I might find him!" cried Job. "That I might come even to his seat! I would order my cause before him. . . .I would know the words which he would answer me, and understand what he would say unto me" (Job 23:3-5).

Prayer is not vague; it is real; it creates. Prayer reaches beyond time; it deals with the eternal realms. Its effects are far-reaching.

The nature of prayer is given in 1 Timothy 2:1: "I exhort therefore, that, first of all, supplications, prayers, intercessions, and giving of thanks, be made for all men." Let us examine these forms of prayer.

Deesis

The Greek word translated "supplication" is *deesis*. The word means humble entreaty, petition. Intense asking, begging, is implied. Prayer is an indication that God is stirring within us concerning some special need. When we pray "in the Holy Ghost," God is manifesting himself. When we are living in Christ, He thinks, wills, and sees through us in our normal daily lives. Supplication is through us of or by the Spirit.

Supplication is the prayer of one who has no right to come to God except with a plea for mercy. Supplication is the prayer that sinners can pray for themselves. That was the prayer of the publican: "God be merciful to me a sinner" (Luke 18:13). It is the prayer that believers can pray for unbelievers. No other prayer will avail other than an appeal for God's mercy toward those who sin.

The following passages use the word *supplication:*

Praying always with all prayer and supplication in the Spirit (Ephesians 6:18).

In everything by prayer and supplication with thanksgiving let your requests be made known unto God (Philippians 4:6).

[Continue] in supplications and prayers (1 Timothy 5:5).

The disciples in the Upper Room "continued with one accord in prayer and supplication" (Acts 1:14).

Proseuche

The Greek word translated "prayers" in 1 Timothy 2:1 is *proseuche.* It is used only of prayer addressed to God. Examples are:

But we will give ourselves continually to prayer (Acts 6:4).

Thy prayers . . . are come up for a memorial before God (Acts 10:4).

Continue in prayer, and watch in the same with thanksgiving (Colossians 4:2).

. . . golden vials full of odors, which are the prayers of the saints (Revelation 5:8).

This is not the petition of a beggar, but the request of one who has a right to make that request. It is prayer based on confidence because of a relationship. Prayer in all its forms is a testimony to God's greatness and our need of Him.

Enteuxis

The next word in 1 Timothy 2:1 is "intercessions." The Greek word is *enteuxis,* meaning a meeting with,

27

an interview, or a conference. More specifically it means to mediate between persons, to plead in behalf of another. It is the prayer of one who is willing to take the place of the one for whom he is praying. The Holy Spirit is an indwelling intercessor (Romans 8:27), and Christ is the great example of intercession "at the right hand of God" (Romans 8:34; Hebrews 7:25).

Intercession is prayer that is born of compassion and nurtured by the Holy Spirit. When we enter into intercessory prayer, we employ heaven's closed circuit of communication. The current of God's matchless love flows through our hearts and back to Him in loving intercession for others.

Where words may fail in dealing with another about his spiritual needs, where personal entreaty may be rejected, there is an avenue open to the believer. We can intercede. Our Lord has been making intercession for us at the Father's throne for nearly 2,000 years. And we are His partners!

Becoming a Middleman

> Which of you shall have a friend, and shall go unto him at midnight, and say unto him, Friend, lend me three loaves; For a friend of mine in his journey is come to me, and I have nothing to set before him? (Luke 11:5,6).

In this parable of the three friends there is an intriguing picture of God's middleman. There I am, standing between two others, both of them my friends.

One of the greatest ways of serving both God and others is to pray. While it is not the only thing, it is the most important. Jesus is showing us a lesson that reaches beyond the *importunity* of a petitioning friend to see the *opportunity* as a man in the middle.

28

On the one hand, I have one tired, hungry friend. On the other hand, I have a rich Friend with unlimited resources. The one has the need; the other has the resources. But I am the key. The needy one depends on me, the middleman. *LOOSE IN HEAVEN*

Relationship . . . Responsibility

I DONT HAVE ANYTHING

My situation is like the middleman—"I have nothing to set before him." But I must not leave it there. "Sorry, but I don't know what to do," is not enough. I have a *significant* relationship to the rich Friend and a *subsequent* responsibility.

Compassion . . . Confidence

The ministry of intercession is based on *compassion* for the one who needs help and *confidence* in the One who is able and willing to help.

In the parable the middleman came at midnight, a most inopportune hour. You don't go knocking at a stranger's door in the middle of the night. But confidence in a friend makes it possible. What a challenge to us as middlemen.

Intercession has been exercised by many of God's greats. Abraham pled for his nephew Lot who was entangled in Sodom's sinful snares. Moses interceded for his people when God was about to consume them (Exodus 32)—one of the greatest prayers of intercession ever recorded. Daniel prostrated himself upon the floor of a Babylonian palace for his people. And the great example is our Lord.

Not a Perfunctory Act

Paul described his prayers for the Galatians as soul

travail (Galatians 4:19). Human inability is aided by the work of the Spirit to fulfill this middleman task.

> Likewise the Spirit also helpeth our infirmities: for we know not what we should pray for as we ought: but the Spirit itself maketh intercession for us with groanings which cannot be uttered (Romans 8:26; also verse 27).

"Talking to men for God is a great thing," declared E. M. Bounds, "but talking to God for men is greater still." Intercession is placing emphasis on others, rather than self. Care for others is the badge of those who travel this lonely path.

Centuries ago the prophet "wondered that there was no intercessor" (Isaiah 59:16). John Knox prayed, "Give me Scotland or I die." Evan Roberts pled for Wales, and we have the record of the great Welsh revival. "Praying Hyde" breathed out his life in prayer for India. Are you willing to give yourself to this ministry?

Eucharistia

The fourth expression is "giving of thanks." Translated from the Greek word *eucharistia*, it means just that—giving of thanks. One of the most neglected aspects of our prayer life is thanksgiving. Do you enter into the Lord's presence, pour out your requests, and then leave?

The Bible exhorts us: "Enter into his gates with thanksgiving, and into his courts with praise: be thankful unto him, and bless his name" (Psalm 100:4). Paul writes to the Philippians: "Be careful for nothing [in nothing be anxious]; but in every thing by prayer and supplication with thanksgiving let your requests be made known unto God" (4:6). And to the Colossians: "Continue in prayer, and watch in the same with thanksgiving" (4:2).

I Will Act

To give thanks requires a definite act of the will. The Psalmist determined: "I will give thanks unto thee for ever" (Psalm 30:12). The "wrath of God is revealed from heaven against all ungodliness and unrighteousness" (Romans 1:18). Among the charges against the apostate unbelievers was: "Because that, when they knew God, they glorified him not as God, neither were thankful" (Romans 1:21).

MOST IMPORTANT

Thanksgiving contributes to a life of freeflowing prayer. Notice the following groupings of exhortations: "Rejoice evermore. Pray without ceasing. In every thing give thanks: for this is the will of God in Christ Jesus concerning you" (1 Thessalonians 5:16-18). Paul prayed for the Roman Christians "without ceasing" and thanked God for them (Romans 1:8,9). The same obtains for the Ephesians (1:15, 16), the Philippians (1:3-11), the Colossians (1:3-12), and the Thessalonians (1 Thessalonians 1:2; 2 Thessalonians 1:3).

Thanksgiving will feed your faith. "O give thanks unto the Lord; call upon his name. . . . Remember his marvelous works that he hath done" (Psalm 105:1,5). Thanksgiving and confidence go together; so do thanksgiving and victory. Thanksgiving is a prelude to victory.

"In every thing give thanks: for this is the will of God in Christ Jesus concerning you" (1 Thessalonians 5:18). There is nothing ambiguous about that. It is the will of God.

31

4

Prayer and the Trinity

"At that time Dr. Jones prayed the most eloquent prayer ever directed to the ears of a Boston audience." Such was the newspaper report of an event at a large religious convention in Boston. The reporter may have been well qualified to write, but he was surely wrong about prayer. Prayer is not directed to the ears of an audience. Humans are not recipients of the prayers; they are recipients of the answers.

How many times my soul has been enriched as others have offered public prayer. They have led me into the very presence of God. Sadly, other prayers have brought little blessing.

The Preposition Is Important

Some men pray *before men* rather than *before God*. They pray to make an impression.

Others pray *to* men. They wish to give out information, share doctrinal exposition, or even inject announcements in their public prayers.

Some pray *at* men. They attempt to correct the faults of others by this means.

Then there are those choice saints who pray *for* men. This is scriptural. It brings blessing, is pleasing to

God, and is profitable for the one who prays and the one for whom prayer is offered.

The Question

But then the question arises: To whom shall we address our prayers? the Father? Jesus? the Holy Spirit? This may sound like a very elementary question, but it is one to which many people apparently give little thought.

First, however, let us look at another phase of prayer form. Should we address God in the second or third person? Frequently we hear expressions such as this: "Oh, Lord, we ask for God's Spirit to minister to us today." Or, "Oh, Lord, may the Spirit be present in God's house today." Would I converse with my brother in this fashion: "Orville, I am glad to be in Orville's home"? Of course not. I would say, "your home."

The model prayer which Jesus gave to His disciples illustrates the point. The disciples were instructed to begin with "Our Father," followed by "Hallowed be thy name." The prayer was addressed to God and it was not, "Hallowed be God's name." Further, it was not "God's kingdom come, God's will be done." In prayer we talk *to* God, not *about* Him. We would do well to keep in mind that we are to focus our attention on God. We are communicating with Him.

Don't Be Bound

My purpose at this point is not to place a person under bondage when he prays in public. God knows and sees our sincerity. But while many are little concerned with theological propriety, it seems that we would do well to understand what the Scriptures teach about proper prayer form.

Now to come back to the question: "To whom shall we address our prayers?" The usual answer is that we should pray to God. Yes, that is correct. But we have a triune God—Father, Son, and Holy Spirit—three Persons in the one Godhead. To which of these three should we address our petitions? Often you hear all three being addressed interchangeably in one prayer.

The Trinity is involved in your prayer life. Father, Son, and Holy Spirit are involved in your salvation and multitudes of benefits. Note among other things these three rich truths: (1) the Father hears your prayers; (2) the Son prays for you at the Father's right hand; and (3) the Holy Spirit prays through you as you permit Him.

Does it make any difference whether we pray to the Father, to the Son, or to the Holy Spirit? The Bible outlines a formula: We pray to our Father, in the name of Jesus Christ our Saviour, through the power of the indwelling Holy Spirit—on the basis that entrance has been opened to us through the blood of Christ (Hebrews 10:19,20).

Praying to the Father

The logical and scriptural Person to whom we address our prayers is God the Father, the First Person of the Godhead. Jesus stated: "In that day ye shall ask me nothing. Verily, verily, I say unto you, Whatsoever ye shall ask the Father in my name, he will give it you" (John 16:23). He also declared: "Whatsoever ye shall ask of the Father in my name, he may give it you" (John 15:16).

We come to God the Father on the basis of what

34

Jesus did. He revealed God as "Father." John declares: "No man hath seen God at any time; the only begotten Son, which is in the bosom of the Father, he hath declared him" (John 1:18.) The word translated "declared" is the word from which we get our English word *exegesis,* which means to reveal or make known.

Always the Father

How great the revelation that Christ gave us when He revealed God as "Father"! The first recorded utterance of Jesus concerned His Father—"Wist ye not that I must be about my Father's business?" (Luke 2:49). His last cry from the cross was, "Father, into thy hands I commend my spirit," and "he gave up the ghost" (Luke 23:46).

Jesus always addressed God as Father. The one exception is found in Mark 15:34: "My God, my God, why hast thou forsaken me?" (cf. Matthew 27:46). In every other instance He never addressed God as God. He calls God "Father" 140 times in the Gospel of John; 48 times in chapters 13-17; 23 in chapter 14 alone.

Jesus' idea of God was more than the conception of Him as a Creator forming a universe or as a Sovereign laying down decrees. He presented a personal and endearing relationship. The root meaning of "father" is not that of birth or progenitorship; it carries the meaning of one who provides and protects, nourishes and cares.

The Great Example

In the great and matchless 17th chapter of John's Gospel we have a picture of the relationship of God the Father and God the Son which staggers description. Six times Jesus uses the word *Father.* Twice it is

35

qualified—holy Father (v. 11) and righteous Father (v. 25). The bond between the Son and the Father is very close and beautiful, very intimate and tender.

Jesus lifted up His eyes to the eternal home, His own eternal dwelling place and said, "Father." And we who know Him and believe on Him as the Son of God and our Saviour can lift up our eyes and say with Jesus, "Father." The God and Father of our Lord Jesus Christ is our God and our Father.

All true prayer must be based on relationship. A repentant sinner and a forgiving God makes pardon possible. We are not sons of God by nature. We were born in sin and alienated from God by guilt as we grew up. We became sons of God through the new birth and the gracious act of "adoption" into His family. Jesus is the "only begotten Son" (John 3:16). He is unique. But through His shed blood we have been "made . . . accepted in the beloved" (Ephesians 1:6). God is our Father as fully as He is His Son's Father.

Praying in Jesus' Name

Jesus said, "If ye shall ask any thing in my name, I will do it." Our position in Christ is real and embraces all that makes our prayers effective. God the Father has accepted us in Christ, the Beloved (Ephesians 1:6). He loves us, honors us, and employs us as sons because we have been made His sons in Christ Jesus. "Behold what manner of love the Father hath bestowed upon us, that we should be called the sons of God" (1 John 3:1).

God the Father looks on me in the sinless righteousness of His Son. Through the sacrifice of Christ's shed blood I came boldly to God (Hebrews 10:19). Being in Christ, I am as near to the Father as Christ.

"Made nigh by the blood of Christ" (Ephesians 2:13) and sitting "in heavenly places in Christ Jesus" (Ephesians 2:6), I am at liberty to petition the Father. "He that spared not his own Son, but delivered him up for us all, how shall he not with him also freely give us all things?" (Romans 8:32).

Two Aspects

There are two aspects of our relationship to Christ in redemption. We are "in Christ" and Christ is "in us." Paul uses both expressions. "Therefore if any man be in Christ, he is a new creature" (2 Corinthians 5:17); and, "Christ liveth in me" (Galatians 2:20).

The Father always hears the Son. If I am in Christ, the Father has His ear tuned my way too. Because of what Jesus Christ accomplished for us at Calvary, we enjoy a greater blessing than even the high priest in the Old Testament. He went into the Most Holy Place once a year, but we are now admitted into the very presence of God at any time. No longer is there a barrier raised between us and God the Father. Jesus has become the "new and living way to God the Father" (Hebrews 10:19-21). For this reason we are exhorted to "come boldly unto the throne of grace, that we may obtain mercy, and find grace to help in time of need" (Hebrews 4:16). The way has been opened into the holiest. Prayer is a vital and tremendous possibility because of the finished work of Christ on the cross of Calvary.

Power of Attorney

My brother has served overseas as a missionary for many years. I also have a son who is an overseas missionary. Both have given me power of attorney to act on their behalf. The power of attorney authorizes me to sign legal papers and write checks on their accounts.

Think of the power of attorney the Lord Jesus has given us. "And whatsoever ye shall ask in my name, that will I do, that the Father may be glorified in the Son. If ye shall ask any thing in my name, I will do it" (John 14:13,14).

Prayer in the name of Jesus has power with God. The Father is well pleased with His Son (Matthew 3:17; Mark 1:11; Luke 3:22). He always hears Him, and He also always hears the prayer offered in Christ's name. There is a fragrance in the name of Jesus Christ that makes every prayer made in that Name acceptable to the Father.

Funds in the Bank

If I go to a bank in which I have no funds and present a check with my signature, I will receive nothing. Since I have no account my name will be of no avail. But if I go to the bank with a check signed by a depositor, all I need is endorsement by my signature.

I have no account in heaven, no credit, absolutely none, but my Saviour has unlimited credit. I can, in His name, draw on His limitless resources. That is the privilege—the power of attorney—He has given me.

Note three statements regarding the name of Jesus relating to this matter:

1. The name of Jesus represents His authority (Matthew 28:18; Ephesians 1:20-22; Philippians 2:9; Hebrews 2:14).

2. The name of Jesus represents His worthiness (Matthew 3:17; John 8:29; Hebrews 7:26; 1 John 2:1, 2).

3. The name of Jesus avails in prayer (John 14:13, 14; 15:16; 16:23, 24).

Praying in the Spirit

> Likewise the Spirit also helpeth our infirmities: for we know not what we should pray for as we ought: but the Spirit itself maketh intercession for us with groanings which cannot be uttered (Romans 8:26).

Prayer inspired and directed by God the Holy Spirit is prayer that God the Father answers. While we do not know how to pray and what to pray for, Jesus promised a Holy Helper, the blessed Holy Spirit (John 14:16, 17). The Holy Helper helps us in our infirmities.

Active but Ineffective

We can be energetically active in our attempts to serve God and yet find ourselves spiritually ineffective. That is the subtle plan of our enemy the devil. The Spirit does not supplement our work or make up for our failures. Nor does He second our efforts. He must be the predominant partner. The words of Acts 15:28 illustrate the point: "For it seemed good to the Holy Ghost, and to us." He must come first.

We may suffer from an inability to be articulate, a poverty of expression, an incoherency in petitioning, but we have this Holy Helper who will come to our aid. May we always recognize and seek His partnership. He will give expression.

The Holy Spirit never tires; He never sinks into routine. He comes to create our prayers, to energize our praying, and to sustain us as we pray. He keeps us out of ruts in our prayer life by leading us into great times of worship, adoration, praise, and thanksgiving. "We . . . worship by the Spirit of God" (Philippians 3:3, *American Standard Version*).

As we pray in the Spirit, He will teach us not only to worship, but also to relate our praying to the Word of God. Note that the exhortation to take the "sword of the Spirit, which is the word of God" is followed by "praying always with all prayer and supplication in the Spirit" (Ephesians 6:17, 18). Taking the sword of the Spirit and praying in the Spirit are linked inseparably. An effective prayer ministry and a life saturated with the Word go hand in hand. Allow the Spirit to mold your prayers by the Word, and you will experience liberty and power in prayer. Without His help your prayer life will be lifeless, formal, and wearisome.

Yes, the Trinity is involved in our prayer life. God the Father hears our prayers; God the Son provides our authority in prayer and prays for us. God the Holy Spirit prompts us to pray and prays in and through us. "Let us therefore come boldly unto the throne of grace."

May the "grace of the Lord Jesus Christ, and the love of God, and the communion of the Holy Ghost, be with you all. Amen" (2 Corinthians 13:14).

5

Attitudes During Prayer

Raphael the painter used to wear a candle in a pasteboard cap, so that, while he was painting, his shadow would not fall on his work. How often our prayers are spoiled by our own shadows.

Our attitudes are of great importance if we are to pray effectively. Prayer is such a costly privilege that we can expect God to have some rules concerning it. And He does.

Prayer begins with necessity, moves to certainty, and ends with ability. Prayer was as vital to Jesus as breathing. He found it necessary to pray. He approached the Father with confidence, and the results are a testimony worthy of our emulation.

The prayer that approaches God in confidence and develops patience while waiting, always ends with success and praise! "He that cometh to God must believe that he is, and that he is a rewarder of them that diligently seek him" (Hebrews 11:6).

Three Types of Prayer

Prayer may be looked at from three different viewpoints:

1. Prayer that is worship, adoration, and communion, without any thought of asking for anything.

41

2. Prayer for personal needs, asking for God's will and favor in our own lives.

3. Prayer for others that the will of God might be done in their lives.

Principles to Follow

The key to power in prayer is to follow certain Biblical principles. These principles worked for the patriarchs and prophets of the Old Testament and for the apostles and saints of the New Testament. They have been consistently effective throughout the Church Age. And, thank God, believing prayer with accompanying answers is not limited to prophets and apostles. The privilege of prayer is the birthright of the humblest child of God.

The *first principle* is to begin with a right relationship with God. We are to approach God with a filial spirit, for we pray to "our Father." Jesus used the word *Father* some 163 times in the Gospels. Fifty-three times it is *My Father*. Seventeen times He addresses God in prayer as "My Father."

The *second principle* is to maintain the relationship free from sin and selfish motives. Sin mars fellowship with God and robs us of victory. "If I regard iniquity in my heart, the Lord will not hear me" (Psalm 66:18). And again:

> Who shall ascend into the hill of the Lord? Or who shall stand in his holy place? He that hath clean hands, and a pure heart; who hath not lifted up his soul unto vanity, nor sworn deceitfully. He shall receive the blessing from the Lord, and righteousness from the God of his salvation (Psalm 24:3-5).

Paul practiced a "conscience void of offense toward God, and toward men" (Acts 24:16).

42

The *third principle* is to pray in faith. Faith is the lifeblood of prayer. Faith and prayer are inextricably interwoven: "Without faith it is impossible to please [God], for he that cometh to God must believe . . . that he is a rewarder of them that diligently seek him" (Hebrews 11:6). There it is—hopelessly entangled, beyond separation.

Lie or Rely

To be consistently successful in the ministry of prayer, you must never doubt or lack confidence in the ultimate outcome of your petition. Maintain a believing mind at all times. A mind filled with conflicting doubts insults the integrity of God by implying that He does not keep His Word. Nurture your faith in God's Word with complete confidence in God (Romans 8:17). We lie to God in prayer if we do not rely on Him after praying.

What is prayer to you? Is it a comforting exercise or a crusade against evil for the honor of God's name? Is it a catalog of personal needs or prevailing petitions for the needs of others? G. Campbell Morgan said: "Men only pray with prevailing power who do so amid the sobs and sighing of the race."

Coming in Humility

Effective praying relates to our attitudes. Examine some basic attitudes with me. First, let us think about humility. Effective prayer means that some things must go—like pride, unkindness, self-importance, self-indulgence.

Jesus gave two parables on prayer in Luke 18:1-14. The first one—the parable of the unjust judge—teaches that prayer should be regular and consistent.

43

The second—the parable of the Pharisee and the publican—teaches that our petitions are never granted on the basis of our merit. Personal unworthiness and true humility of spirit are prerequisites of effective prayer.

An Insult

Self-sufficiency is a horrible insult to God. The parable was directed toward those who "trusted in themselves that they were righteous, and despised others" (Luke 18:9).

The Pharisee and the publican were two opposite characters. The Pharisee was a religious man; the publican, a sinner. The contrast was extreme. The Pharisee embodied religious pride; giving attention to externals, seeking the honor of men, and showing a condescending attitude to God.

The Pharisee prayed with himself. He addressed himself to God, but he directed his prayers toward himself. His eyes and his mind were on himself as he stood in a conspicuous place to be seen and heard of men. He went to pray, but instead, did nothing but praise himself and condemn others. His feelings of merit were drawn from the demerit of others. With his mind on his own moral excellence, he seemed to say, "God, I'm a spiritual masterpiece, religiously proper. You are fortunate to have me praying."

A Lesson I Learned

A personal experience is indelibly stamped in my memory. Standing by the hospital bedside of a dear and godly friend, I began to pray for him. Proceeding to tell God of the greatness of this man, I was suddenly checked by the Holy Spirit. This man had been a leader greatly used of God, and I was sincere in my eulogy. He had contributed so much to me and a host of others. But the Spirit checked me so forcibly that I stopped praying. Calling the man by name, I said, "I feel rebuked by the Holy Spirit for pleading your cause on the basis of your worthiness." He readily agreed, and I began again on the basis of our Lord's worthiness. It was a lesson I will not forget.

The parable teaches us that we must come to God on the merits of the Lord Jesus Christ. To come on the basis of our goodness is obnoxious to God. We tend to overrate ourselves. Our righteousness comes only by virtue of Christ's merit. The Pharisee was not justified before God: "For every one that exalteth himself shall be abased." But the publican went home justified. The man who justified himself remained unjustified. The man who sought the compassion of God went back to his house justified. We can come with confidence, but we must plead our place humbly as Blood-bought children of God.

Forgive and Be Forgiven

Consider now the attitude of forgiveness. In the model prayer that our Lord gave there is a vital petition, "Forgive us . . . as we forgive." How can we accept forgiveness so richly given and at the same time withhold forgiveness from others? It is a forgiving heart that seeks and receives God's forgiveness.

C. S. Lewis once quipped: "Everyone says forgiveness is a lovely idea, until they have something to forgive." Unforgiveness is a luxury Christians can't afford. An unforgiving spirit grows like a choking weed in the soil of our souls.

Four Sides

There are really *four sides* to forgiveness. *First,* there is God's forgiveness of us. This forgiveness came at the cost of the death of His only begotten Son at Calvary.

The *second side* is our forgiveness of ourselves. "If we confess our sins, he is faithful and just to forgive us our sins, and to cleanse us from all unrighteousness" (1 John 1:9). Believe God's promise and you will forgive yourself. For years Tom Anderson's life was plagued by the memory of a fraternity escapade that caused the death of a classmate. He lost job after job. After 6 years of marriage, he and his wife separated. Then something happened. Life began anew. This is his story.

> For years I thought, "Nothing can undo what I've done." The thought of my guilt would stop me in the middle of a smile or a handshake. It put a wall between others and me. Then I had an unexpected visit from the person I dreaded most to see—the mother of the classmate who died.
>
> "Years ago," she said, "I found it in my heart, through prayer, to forgive you. Your wife forgave you. So did your friends." She paused, and then said sternly, "You are the one person who hasn't forgiven Tom Anderson."
>
> I looked in her eyes and found there a kind of permission to be the person I might have been if her boy had lived. For the first time in my adult life I felt worthy to love and be loved.

The *third side* is that which concerns our relationship with others. God's forgiving and our forgiving others go together (Matthew 5:23, 24; 6:12, 14, 15; 7:2-5; 18:21, 22, 34, 35; Ephesians 4:32; 1 Peter 3:9). If we have God's forgiveness, our gratefulness to Him will be a power within our hearts causing us to forgive others. Resentments, grudges, and hostile feelings must go if we are to experience spiritual, mental, and physical well-being as well as an effective prayer life.

The *fourth side* is to seek the forgiveness of those we have wronged (Matthew 5:23). We must be willing to forgive, and we also need to seek forgiveness when we have been wrong. Two chapters in Matthew present God's standard procedure on forgiveness among Christians. Matthew 5:21-26 deals with the *offender*; Matthew 18 pictures the *offended*. Jesus placed equal responsibility on both. Remember there are times when the shortest road to God is by way of our brother. We are no more right with our Father who is above us than we are with our brother who is beside us.

Prevailing

There is no mistaking the plain teaching of Scripture regarding persevering in prayer. Consider Abraham's boldness and importunity in interceding for Sodom and his nephew Lot. Think of Daniel who "was mourning three full weeks," waiting on God for information regarding the future of Israel.

In an earlier chapter we gave brief consideration to the "middleman"—the man who came to the neighbor's door at midnight to get three loaves. We emphasized his *opportunity*. Now we will emphasize his *importunity*. The reason given for his success was his unabashed holding on until the answer came (Luke 11:5-10).

In the closing verses of this parable, Jesus gave us a triad indicating three degrees of fervency—ask, seek, knock. In the *asking* we have the *privilege* of prayer. In the *seeking* we have the *passion* of prayer. In the *knocking* we have the *perseverance* of prayer.

47

Asking . . . Seeking . . . Knocking

The way to get the thing that is for sale is to pay for it. The way to get a thing that is to be earned is to work for it. The way to get a thing that is to be given is to ask for it.

Ask, and it shall be given you (Matthew 7:7).
How much more shall your Father which is in heaven give good things to them that ask him? (Matthew 7:11).
Whatsoever ye shall ask in my name that will I do (John 14:13).
If ye shall ask . . . I will do it (John 14:14).

Make it a practice to ask God first before you seek human help.

To seek implies a treasure awaiting discovery. The word *seek* has a world of meaning in the Bible. A wealthy reward awaits those who will make the effort to study its usage and meaning.

To knock implies necessity of effort. The benefits of prayer are for those who will not be denied. Prevailing prayer involves unceasing prayer. We are instructed to "pray without ceasing" (1 Thessalonians 5:17). Paul issues as a command what Christ presented as a duty. "Men ought always to pray, and not to faint" (Luke 18:1). To faint means "to lose heart."

Persevering in Prayer

When God tells us to pray with perseverance, He uses the word *continue*. The word is used in Acts 2:46 where the early believers were "continuing daily . . . with singleness of heart." It appears again in Acts 10:7 where it describes the singleness of purpose of Cornelius' soldier—to wait on Cornelius' every wish and every command.

Jesus used the word *importunity* (Luke 11:8), which means literally "shamelessness." Implied is a determination not to be put to shame by a seeming refusal, but to exercise holy boldness.

This does not mean we are to badger God to be heard. He is not an ingracious deity who must be forced into compliance (Luke 18:7, 8). Yet perseverance in prayer is a proof of sincerity. Can God be moved by words that do not move us?

Vagueness Is Laziness

Prayer should have purpose. Vague praying is lazy praying. We don't go into the meat market and ask for 5 pounds of meat. We specify chuck roast, ground round, lamb, pork chops, etc. The seamstress designates the kind of cloth—cotton, wool, polyester, silk—not just 3 yards of cloth. God will specifically answer specific prayers.

In the Will of God

Closely related to importunity and specificity in prayer must be the desire for God's will. "This is the confidence that we have . . . , if we ask any thing according to his will, he heareth us" (1 John 5:14). The word *confidence* can be translated "free-spokenness." Praying in His will makes us free to speak to our Heavenly Father.

It is impossible to have faith that can remove mountains without the knowledge of God's will. By submitting our hearts, searching His Word, and waiting on Him we are able to find His will. We need to learn to walk in the Spirit, to be led by the Spirit. The Spirit will help us (Romans 8:26, 27). Haste is the parent of the majority of our mistakes concerning the

49

will of God. The man who rushes ahead without patience has many steps to wearily retrace. The man who waits has few. When in doubt, wait.

Come to God with an *unaffected approach*, in simplicity and sincerity (the "true heart" of Hebrews 10:22).

Come to God with *unforced words* like the publican of Luke 18.

Come to God with *unfeigned faith* like the father of the boy with the dumb spirit of Mark 9:24. Simplicity and humility walk hand in hand. Nothing lies beyond the reach of prayer except that which is outside the will of God.

Come to God with *uncluttered wants,* praying as our Lord prayed, "Thy will be done" (Matthew 26:39, 42, 44).

6

Biblical Instances of Answered Prayer

"I shall never believe in prayer again," said a brokenhearted girl. "If anyone prayed in faith, I prayed that my mother might recover. But she died. Oh, how could God be so cruel?"

Wisely her friend answered, "There are few deaths, thank God, where no one present prays that the loved one may live. Do you suppose that the gift of prayer was given us in order that no one may ever die? Do you think God intended men to live on in growing infirmity, until at last they prayed for death? Prayer is a blessing because God knows best how to answer."

Throw Out the Phone?

We don't get what we want every time we pick up the spiritual telephone of prayer anymore than we get what we want every time we pick up the phone in our home or office. But if we don't get the response we want, we don't throw the phone out! Neither should we throw our spiritual phone away just because we don't get what we want.

But God does respond to our prayers with positive answers. The Bible is replete with great accounts of victories won through effectual prayer. "The effectual fervent prayer of a righteous man availeth much" (James 5:16).

51

They Prayed ... God Answered

Abraham's servant prayed and Rebekah was the answer (Genesis 24). Moses prayed and a nation was saved from death. Joshua prayed and the sun stood still. Hannah prayed and God gave her a son. Solomon prayed for wisdom and God made him the wisest of men. Jehoshaphat prayed and God turned away His anger. Elijah prayed and the sacrifice was consumed. Elisha prayed and received a double portion. Hezekiah prayed and the sundial was turned back. Mordecai prayed and the Jews were spared. Daniel prayed and the jaws of the lions were locked. Paul and Silas prayed, and the prison shook, the doors opened, and their chains fell off. Peter prayed and Dorcas came alive. The thief prayed and went with Christ to paradise. And on and on the record could be recited.

Esau wrestled with wild animals and brought home venison; Jacob wrestled with angels and brought home glory. There were many contrasts in these two brothers, but nothing was so contrasting as their rewards. Esau gained favor wth Isaac; Jacob gained favor with God.

"The Holy Ghost," stated E. M. Bounds, "does not flow through methods, but through men . . . . He does not anoint plans, but men—men of prayer."

Prayers and Pray-ers

Study the great prayers of the Bible and the great pray-ers, and you will find answers to a host of questions. What should we pray for? How should we pray? Where should we pray? Who can pray? Why should we pray?

Abraham, the friend of God, was a man of prayer. He had no trouble making contact with heaven. Again and again God spoke and Abraham responded. From the time he left Ur of the Chaldees until his earthly tabernacle was laid away in the tomb at age 175, Abraham was a man of the altar. Whenever and wherever he stopped in his journeys, he "called upon the name of the Lord."

Much could be written about his times of prayer — falling on his face as God talked to him about the promised son Isaac; his prevailing prayer for healing for Abimelech and his family (Genesis 20:17); his prayer for Ishmael (Genesis 17:18, 20). But the prayer I wish to dwell on is Abraham's intercession for Sodom.

The Bible says God *knew* Abraham (Genesis 18:19). God knew Abraham would order his family in His ways. The word translated "know" from the Hebrew can also be translated "chosen" or "made . . . my friend." How amazing! God chose to share His plan with Abraham. He was about to wipe Sodom off the face of the earth.

Then followed Abraham's intercession:

> Will you kill good and bad alike? Suppose you find fifty godly people . . . ? . . . forty-five? . . . forty? . . . thirty? . . . twenty? . . . ten? (Genesis 18:24-32, *The Living Bible*).

But there weren't even 10. Only his nephew Lot and Lot's family were spared. Possibly the greatest lesson for Abraham was his discovery that a righteous God would spare Sodom if there were only 10 righteous people in the city. Sodom was not spared, but Abraham had a new understanding of a just and righteous God who also would deal in mercy.

Transformed Trickster

Turning to Genesis 32 we take a look at Jacob. All of

53

his life he had resorted to trickery. With the aid of his mother he had conned his twin brother Esau out of his birthright. Because of Esau's rage Jacob was forced to flee from home, only to spend many lonesome years in a strange land.

During Jacob's flight he had a significant encounter with God. As he slept alone under the stars one night, God made a series of covenant promises in a dream (Genesis 28). There Jacob covenanted with God (v. 22) and named the place Bethel (the house of God).

Arriving at his destination in Haran, Jacob began working for his uncle Laban. Despite God's promise of future wealth in land and descendants and the promise of His presence and protection, Jacob resorted to trickery. By every means possible he would further his own ends. But he met his match in Laban who tricked Jacob by giving him Leah as his wife instead of Rachel, the girl whom he loved. During his 14 years of servitude (paying) for two wives and then under a new partnership arrangement, Jacob prospered. His life was ruled by greed, but plagued by fear and family troubles. Finally Jacob with his family and possessions fled while Laban was away.

Plotting, Planning, or Praying?

Jacob now faced another crisis. With the prospect of disaster at the hands of Esau whom he had not seen for years and whose wrath he greatly feared, he plotted and planned. Jacob was the supplanter, the man who looked out for himself and schemed to gain what God had promised. Frantic with fear, Jacob prayed (Genesis 32:9-12).

Do you struggle with fears and uncertainties? Do

you plan and plan and plan? Do you lie awake at night trying to work your way out? Turn to God in prayer.

Victorious Defeat

At Jabbok's ford Jacob had a life-changing experience. He wrestled with a man until daybreak. Picture the struggle that goes on during the hours of darkness. Terrified, but unyielding, he continues. All of his life he has had to fight or flee. No one can be trusted. Suddenly at daybreak Jacob is crippled. Searing pain races through his leg—it's useless. His opponent cries, "Let me go, for it is dawn."

Realization comes to Jacob. The wrestler is more than a human. And he answers, "I will not let you go until you bless me." And there Jacob receives a new name, no longer the supplanter, but Israel, the prince. As the streaks of dawn lit up the eastern sky, Jacob named the place Peniel (the face of God), and proceeded on his way to his homeland with a limp in his step—a limp that would be a lifelong reminder. There at Jabbok a "victorious defeat" had been experienced.

Mighty Intercessor

Moses won recognition by God because of his intercession: "And the Lord said unto Moses, I will do this thing also that thou hast spoken: for thou hast found grace in my sight, and I know thee by name" (Exodus 33:17). For 40 days and nights without food or water Moses pressed for the salvation of God's people, and God changed His mind and spared them (Exodus 32:11-14).

Only hours later Moses sought the Lord again in one of the greatest prayers of intercession ever recorded:

> And Moses returned unto the Lord, and said, Oh, this people have sinned a great sin. . . . Yet now, if thou wilt forgive their sin —; and if not, blot me, I pray thee, out of thy book which thou hast written (Exodus 32:31, 32).

God's plan to let His anger blaze out and destroy the Israelites and His offer to make a great nation from Moses would have tempted some people. Moses had had endless problems, tensions, and worries with the troublesome backsliders. Why not chuck the whole miserable, undisciplined bunch?

But Moses, the man who knew the "ways" of God (Psalm 103:7), pled with God, even to the extent that God, if necessary, would blot out his name to spare Israel. He freely admitted the abhorrence of their sin; there were no excuses, no condemnation, only an appeal for mercy. And God was merciful.

Not a Special Breed

Many people believe that God's greats of the past were like a special piece of machinery. They were not; they were men of like passions. The secret—they prayed. Moses was timid and fearful. He led Israel, not out of personal ambition, but because God called him. And God is calling yet today. He wants you. He wants you to hold Him to His Word. Do you know what that Word is?

Child of Prayer

Samuel came into the world because of a praying mother. Born of a praying mother, his first months were under the influence of her prayers. "Lent to the Lord" by his godly mother, Samuel early in life left home to serve in the tabernacle. His mother's prayers followed him there.

56

That mother, Hannah, had a problem that was magnified by the society of her day where men kept more than one wife. She was barren and had to endure the ridicule and disrespect of her rival. Her burden seemed more than she could bear, but she took the right course. She laid the matter before the Lord in earnest supplication (1 Samuel 1). How often we moan and groan about our plight instead of going to the One who has the answer.

God hears the earnest cry of an agonizing soul. He responds with more than a pacifier or a toy. He meets the heart's cry. He met Hannah's need and gave her a son. That son became one of the great leaders in Israel's history. He, in turn, became a prayer warrior. Living in a day when "every man did that which was right in his own eyes," Samuel learned early to serve God. He stands as a bright light in a dark period of Israel's life. Alone he stood before God for a nation in need.

Like Produces Like

Praying Samuels come from praying Hannahs. Samuel's prayer life was born in the prayers of his mother and in her obedience to God. His life of prayer grew out of obedience to God's Word and increasing knowledge of Him. Men with power in prayer build the framework of careful, consistent obedience to the Word of God.

Samuel's prayers and preaching brought repentance, but the Israelites still felt their weakness. As the Philistines came against them, they turned to Samuel: "Cease not to cry unto the Lord our God for us, that he will save us . . . "(1 Samuel 7:8).

Samuel became known in heaven as a man of

prayer. Hundreds of years after Samuel's death, God himself referred to Samuel's powerful intercession (Jeremiah 15:1). Moses and Samuel were the intercessors who turned away God's wrath in times of Israel's sin and declension.

The Tishbite

> Elijah was a man subject to like passions as we are, and he prayed earnestly that it might not rain: and it rained not . . . three years and six months. And he prayed again, and the heaven gave rain (James 5:17, 18).

Elijah was a Tishbite. But what is a Tishbite? A Tishbite was an inhabitant of Tishbeh, an isolate, obscure area of Gilead, kind of a "no place." Elijah was a "nobody." He was one of that company of "nobodies" whom God used to do great exploits.

Elijah the Tishbite, at home in desert wastes and mountain caves, was entirely detached from the ostentatious society of his day. His style of dress was not the latest, and his approach was straight from the shoulder.

While his biography is brief, it speaks volumes. It can be reduced to two words—"He prayed." From James we note three things: (1) Elijah "was as completely human as we are"; (2) he prayed and there was no rain for 3½ years; (3) he prayed again and the heavens opened.

Elijah was divinely and miraculously fed by ravens in time of drought. By faith he caused a widow's food supply to be miraculously multiplied. He prayed and her son was brought back from the dead. Of all the amazing events in Elijah's ministry, none was more dramatic than the fire called down from heaven on Mt. Carmel. Miracle after miracle marked his life, in-

cluding the startling way in which his career ended as
he was taken to glory without seeing death.

The Ordinary Made Extraordinary

Yes, Elijah came out of obscurity, and centuries
later the New Testament writer marks the significance
of his life and ministry as simply "he prayed." Note
three things about his prayers:

(1) He prayed earnestly. A good translation of
James 5:17 can be: "Elijah with all his passions prayed
in his prayer." As a jet engine turns a contrary wind
into additional lift-and-thrust, so Elijah turned every
adversity into lift-and-thrust by prayer.

(2) He prayed specifically. Stepping out in naked
faith, he could not have been more specific—or ex-
posed. We often are not specific, because we hedge in
unbelief (James 1:6, 7).

(3) He prayed with God's glory in focus (1 Kings
18:36, 37). Do your prayers have that focus? Or are
they totally self-motivated?

Elijah, a most eccentric prophet, portrays not what
a great man can do for God, but what God can do
through an ordinary person. The ordinary made extra-
ordinary by the Spirit can shake the world.

Space does not permit us to tell of the many
instances of answered prayer. Note quickly the
following:

The sun stood still for a day in answer to Joshua's
prayer (Joshua 10:12, 13). Jonah was delivered from
the belly of the fish (Jonah 2).

The first recorded apostolic miracle was: "In the
name of Jesus Christ of Nazareth rise up and walk"

(Acts 3:6). And the cripple rose as Peter lifted him; he was perfectly healed.

And again Peter "kneeled down, and prayed" (Acts 9:40), and the saintly Dorcas was raised from the dead. "Paul and Silas prayed and sang praises unto God" (Acts 16:25), even though their backs were bleeding and they were bound in stocks in the Philippian jail. God answered with an earthquake that shook the foundations and opened the doors, freeing the prisoners. Paul prayed and the father of Publius was healed (Acts 28:8, 9). Paul's fasting and prayer gave him God's assurance that every life would be spared following the 2 weeks' nightmare of the terrible storm at sea. While the ship was shattered to bits, all 276 aboard were spared.

More Hall of Famers

Daniel, Shadrach, Meshach, and Abednego "stood in the gap." Through prayer they "subdued kingdoms, wrought righteousness, obtained promises, stopped the mouths of lions, quenched the violence of fire" (Hebrews 11:33, 34). Think of Ezra and his friends fasting and praying at the river Ahava, finding the right way, and obtaining God's special favor for a whole nation. Job prayed and the Lord restored his wealth and happiness, giving him twice as much as before.

Joshua prayed and the walls of Jericho fell. David prayed and Goliath of Gath dropped dead. He prayed again and Ahithophel hanged himself. Joseph prayed and was exalted to be prime minister of Egypt. Hagar prayed and the angel of the Lord appeared. Nehemiah prayed and the king's heart was softened. Elisha prayed and Jordan was divided. The disciples prayed and Christ stilled the storm. Bartimaeus cried to Jesus and received his sight. The publican prayed and went down to his house justified.

Jesus prayed for Peter that his faith would not fail. The church prayed for Peter, and he was miraculously delivered from prison. Stephen prayed and Saul of Tarsus could not forget it. Cornelius prayed and Peter brought the message of salvation to his house, and Cornelius and his household became the first Gentiles to receive the baptism in the Holy Spirit. Paul and Silas prayed and the Philippian jailer and his household were saved.

With the writer of Hebrews I say:

> And what shall I more say? for the time would fail me to tell of Gideon, and of Barak, and of Samson, and of Jephthah; of David also, and Samuel, and of the prophets (Hebrews 11:32).

God's prayer warriors, though a minority, do not know defeat.

7

Elements of a Personal Devotional Life

A large group of ship radio operators were waiting in the lobby of an employment office; they were there to try out for a job aboard one of the line's ships. Most of them talked with each other, or read magazines. Some of them heard messages in dots and dashes coming over a loudspeaker, but they were all messages for employees in the office, and so they stopped listening and went back to their talk and magazines. All but one man . . . .

This one man suddenly leaped to his feet and went boldly into the inner office. In a few minutes he came back with the announcement that they could all go home now; he had the job! One of the disappointed ones snapped, "You've got your nerve, going in ahead of us. We were here first." To which the other replied, "Any one of you could have had the job if you had been listening."

"What do you mean, listening?"

"I mean listening to the code that came over the loudspeakers. It said, 'The man we want must be alert. The first one to get this message and come immediately into the main office will get the job.' "

Prayer is as much listening as talking.

Your Summit Conference

Prayer can be thought of as a high-level conference with God. Follow these rules for a successful summit conference:

1. Have a simple agenda. Concentrate on adoration, worship, praise, and then specific needs.
2. Be a good listener. Prayer is dialogue. Don't do all the talking. Give God a chance.
3. Watch your motives. Are you only self-centered, or are you concerned about the will and glory of God?

If you read the Bible, you can't help but observe the close connection between the deep prayer life of Jesus and the power of the Holy Spirit which flowed from His life. In the hustle and bustle of His daily life, Jesus often withdrew to be alone with the Father: "And in the morning, rising up a great while before day, he went out, and departed into a solitary place, and there prayed" (Mark 1:35). While alone with the Father, Jesus seemed to find the strength and courage to do the Father's will during His earthly life.

Life without a solitary place is life without a quiet center. There are many things we could never appreciate if it were not for the quiet hours or the stillness. Is there a note of music as effective and powerful as the pause?

Power in Stillness

There are many reasons why we need to be still or quiet. The power of *stillness helps us to know ourselves*. God can't help you determine your real needs until you know something about yourself. He can't help you to know yourself if you are never still. As you know yourself better, it makes you know how much more you need to know God.

Stillness helps us to know God. "Be still, and know that I am God" (Psalm 46:10). The more we know about ourselves, the more we need to know about God. The more we know about God's bigness, the more we realize how small we are. As God becomes bigger in our lives, we become smaller in our own eyes and see ourselves as we really are. As we see God we gain quietness and confidence which is our strength (Isaiah 30:15).

I am told that in the great power-generating plant at Niagara Falls there is a large room different from all the others. In it there isn't a person to be seen, and scarcely a sound to be heard. That room is known as the Still Room. It is the center of the whole operation. The entire operation of producing power to furnish electricity to millions, to turn factory wheels, to manufacture food and clothing, and a hundred and one things—the whole process hinges on what is done there. The Still Room is the center of it all.

Stillness helps us to find our way in the will of God. Busy activity proves nothing. You can't expect to hear God's voice in the midst of the din of life. If your mind churns with confusing emotions—unrest, tension, fear, anger, worry—your spiritual equilibrium will be upset. You'll have a hard time hearing the still small voice behind you saying, "This is the way, walk ye in it" (Isaiah 30:21).

30:15

Too Much Talk

Prayer isn't all talk. We talk too much. We need to become receptive to the voice of God. Cultivate the art of waiting on God. To wait on God is to experience the most intimate and real relationship with Him that anyone has ever known. We come to the point where the Spirit can meet with our spirit. When you wait on God, your spirit gains ascendancy over your flesh. Your whole being comes under the control of the Holy Spirit. You are spiritually minded (Romans 8:6) when you truly wait on the Lord.

> Hast thou not known? hast thou not heard, that the everlasting God, the Lord, the Creator of the ends of the earth, fainteth not, neither is weary? there is no searching of his understanding. He giveth power to the faint; and to them that have no might he increaseth strength.
> *Even youths shall faint and be weary, and the selected young men shall feebly stumble and fall exhausted; But those who wait for the Lord—who expect, look for and hope in Him—shall change and renew their strength and power; they shall lift their wings and mount up [close to God] as eagles [mount up to the sun]; they shall run and not be weary; they shall walk and not faint or become tired* (Isaiah 40:28-31; italicized portion from *The Amplified Bible*).

Aloneness Isn't All Bad

"Alone with God, the world forbidden," wrote the songwriter. Repeatedly we hear that no man lives to himself. That is true. But the opposite statement is equally true and equally important. Periods of solitude—of aloneness—are needed to balance the inner spirit. Somewhere along the way in the pressure of busyness we have lost the art of enjoying aloneness. For the most part we are entertained. We are auditors, or viewers, but seldom participants. Little time is spent alone.

Moses was alone with sheep on "the back side of the desert" when he received the great revelation of the name of God, "I Am That I Am." There at the burning bush he received his commission with the promise that God would deliver Israel.

Jacob was alone on the plains in the middle of the night, a star-studded heaven as a canopy, when God introduced himself and promised the perpetuation of Israel.

John was alone "in the Spirit on the Lord's day" on Rocky Patmos when God gave him the Revelation.

Paul was alone in Arabia when he received much of the great doctrinal truths found in the Epistles.

Our Lord, alone in Gethsemane, prayed in solitude. But He, and all who cultivate such aloneness, are not alone. The Heavenly Father is there.

Solitude in the physical world, and aloneness in the spiritual world, are needed and must be cultivated.

The devotional life is the sole means whereby we get to know God, ourselves, and others. Some picture devotions as primarily feeding one's own spiritual needs. We do feed our soul that way, but devotions must not degenerate into a purely selfish activity of introspection. Your devotions should turn you first to God; they should be a means of bringing you to worship. Whether in prayer or Bible reading, you will want to worship God; finding out what He has to say and learning how to obey Him. You will look at your own life and its needs. And you will become sensitive to the needs of others.

Pray or Prey

The healthiest Christian, the one best fitted for godly living and godly labors, is the one who feeds most on Christ. Faithfulness in Bible reading and prayer constitutes a vitamin-enriched diet. Unless we go apart to wait before God we will come apart. Unless we pray, we will be a prey. Mary of Bethany chose "that good part," to sit and learn at the feet of Jesus (Luke 10:38-42). We develop an "at-home-ness" with God in our devotional life.

One lady tells how she learned the secret of receiving strength for each day:

> I used to get up in a hurry each morning, hasten to the office, and madly rush hour after hour to complete the day's work. Some days were bad, others worse; always, great tension. Then one day I learned a secret. I learned the secret of renewal — sitting a while in silence, waiting before God, thinking of Him as the source of my help, before starting my day's work. This practice did not come easy; but the more I tried it the more poise and strength I received for each of my duties during the day.

Brownie Points

There are people who feel they have fulfilled their obligation to God—really earned brownie points with Him—by attending church services at Christmas and Easter. Others feel that "Now I lay me down to sleep" prayers are enough. Most people pray at some time or another even though some would not want to admit it. A significant expression came out of the horror of the Bataan death march in the Philippines at the outset of World War II—"There were no infidels on Bataan."

"Dailyness" Needed

Occasional prayer is not enough. There must be a "dailyness" about it. "Blessed is the man that heareth me, watching *daily* at my gates, waiting at the posts of my doors. For whoso findeth me findeth life, and shall obtain favor of the Lord" (Proverbs 8:34, 35). Em-

67

phasis is given to the need to *hear*, to *watch*, and to *wait* daily.

Feeding on the Word is more than memorizing Scripture. True, "Man shall not live by bread alone, but by every word that proceedeth out of the mouth of God" (Matthew 4:4). Living on the Word comes by letting that Word speak to your soul in the quiet of meditation and prayer. You can be doctrinally correct but spiritually dead. You need the life of the Spirit igniting the truth of the Word in your heart.

We don't eat a month's supply of food at the beginning of each month. We feed our physical bodies daily. Meals must be prepared, tables set, dishes washed; but that's life. In the same manner we need to daily partake of spiritual food.

Don't Call Me

Some people apparently choose a relationship with God that could be termed a "don't-call-me-I'll-call-you-when-I-need-you" attitude. Thank God, He is always available on the spur of the moment, but He longs to have a vital, continuing relationship.

The life of prayer takes time and discipline. There are some things that just must not be crowded out. There must be some "reserved seats for the soul." The quiet place, the quiet hour, and the quiet heart are the secrets.

"In quietness and in confidence shall be your strength" (Isaiah 30:15). The mightiest forces in the universe are the quiet forces. It is not often that noise and confusion go with strength. Think of the silent power of gravity or electricity.

Someone has given us the following good advice:

68

Slow me down, Lord.

Ease the pounding of my heart by the quieting of my mind.

Steady my hurried pace with a vision of the eternal reach of time.

Give me, amid the confusion of the day, the calmness of the everlasting hills.

Break the tensions of my nerves and muscles with the soothing music of the singing streams that live in my memory. Help me to know the magical, restoring power of sleep.

Teach me the art of taking minute vacations—of slowing down to look at a flower, to chat with a friend, to pat a dog, to read a few lines from a good book.

Slow me down, Lord, and inspire me to send my roots deep into the soil of life's enduring values that I may grow towards the stars of my greater destiny.

The orderly exercise of prayer consists of worship, praise, thanksgiving, confession, petition, supplication, and intercession.

Worth-ship

Worship is the highest and most essential act and experience of a Christian and of a local church. The word *worship* comes from an Anglo-Saxon word which means "worth-ship." To put it simply, worship can be defined as ascribing worth to God. The Psalmist admonishes us: "Give unto the Lord the glory due unto his name" (Psalm 29:2). Worship is portrayed as the Lamb of God is exalted in the glory world: "Worthy is the Lamb that was slain to receive power, and riches, and wisdom, and strength, and honor, and glory, and blessing" (Revelation 5:12).

This dimension of prayer is intrinsic in the very nature of our relationship with God. In worship I quicken my conscience by seeing the holiness of God; I feed my mind by the truth of God; I purge my imagination by the magnificence of God; I open my heart to the love of God; and I devote my will to the purpose of God. It is an encounter with One of worth and excellence; One to whom reverence, respect, and submission are due. True worship will relieve you of the feeling that you are wearily trudging a religious treadmill and harboring the haunting question of what is wrong with your spiritual life.

Response, Not Ritual

Praise should be the natural outcome of a growing relationship with God. Praise is not a ritual but a response to what the Lord has done. The Bible is filled with examples of and exhortations to praise the Lord (Psalm 34:1; Philippians 4:4; Hebrews 13:15; 2 Chronicles 20). Praise God for what He has done, what He is doing, and what He shall do. "In every thing give thanks" (1 Thessalonians 5:18).

At times we may not thank God for specific circumstances, but we can thank Him despite the adverse situation. To illustrate: we would not thank God for the death of an unsaved loved one, but we will praise Him for His wonderful works despite such a tragedy. Never resign yourself to the idea "what will happen, will happen." Let meaningful praise begin in the most discouraging situation. No matter what comes our way, we can offer praise to God and we will discover that praise will bring a release. Learn to experience Christ's lordship in your life.

Thankful . . . Thinkful

The Psalms speak the heart language of thanksgiving. In the old Anglo-Saxon, to be *thankful* meant to

70

be *thinkful*. Paul in Philippians 4:6 urges: "With thanksgiving let your requests be made known unto God."

A missionary was living a defeated life. Everything seemed to be touched with sadness. Although he prayed and prayed for months for victory over depression and discouragement, his life remained the same. He determined to leave his work and go to an interior station to pray till victory came. Arriving at the place, he was welcomed and entertained in the home of a fellow missionary. On the wall hung a motto with the words, "Try Thanksgiving." The words gripped him. He stopped his agonizing in prayer and began to thank God. He was so revolutionized in his outlook that he returned to his post of duty with victory in his life and rich blessing on his ministry. Think and thank!

Preparing for Prayer

Feeding the soul regularly and consistently on the Word of God and coming before the throne of God in worship, adoration, praise, and thanksgiving, bring us to the place of the full range of prayer.

The *prayer of penitence and confession* results from seeing the Lord (Isaiah 6:1-5). The *prayer of aspiration* serves as a stimulus to growth and renewed effort. The *prayer of petition* includes the whole range of our needs and desires; helping us to make right choices, determine a course of action, and live the right way of life. The *prayer of supplication* is one of earnest entreaty, literally begging, based totally on an appeal for mercy. The *prayer of intercession* is a labor of love on behalf of others.

A consistent devotional life will effect dedication

71

and commitment in our lives. Lessons in faith will come, and we will be enabled to pray the prayer of faith. A confident, serene, and quiet spirit will possess our lives. Archbishop Fenelou, one of the geniuses of the devotional life, said: "How rare it is to find a soul quiet enough to hear God speak."

8

Bible Reading and Memorization

Recently a dear friend received a call to a new assignment. His work on earth was completed, and the Master of the harvest called him into His presence. That friend, W.H. Kesler, had spent over 50 years in the ministry. His sterling Christian character and example had been marked by a deep devotional life and a consuming love for the Word of God. An outstanding highlight of his youth was when he and one of his sisters memorized 25 chapters of the Bible. Their reward for this difficult task was a 40-mile train trip, an experience to be remembered fondly at that time in America's history.

Chart and Compass

God's Word was an anchor, chart, compass, and rudder for W.H. Kesler's life. Imagine a great ship at sea without an anchor, chart, compass, or rudder. Utter chaos, shipwreck, and loss would be inevitable.

As tragic as that would be, there is a more far-reaching tragedy all around us. Millions of people sail the sea of life without a chart, compass, rudder, or anchor. They have no anchor for the soul, no chart to indicate their destination, no compass to properly orient their lives, and no rudder of God's guidance to steer a straight course through the turmoil and confusion of life.

Note three things about the relevancy of the Bible to our times:

First, the Bible predicts our times as they are. All the news commentator can do is speculate about the probable course of events. The Bible describes the beginning and the end of human history.

Second, the Bible gives us courage and strength to face our times. There is no other foundation but Christ; no hope, peace, or certainty apart from Him. Wars and rumors of wars are only a part of a world where political, economic, and social ferments point to a possible disaster. He who has his faith rooted in the Word of God sees beyond these uncertainties. He knows that God is sovereign, and all that occurs is permitted by Him.

Third, the Bible promises hope for the future. The hereafter is veiled to the non-Christian, but the Bible pulls aside the veil and reveals bits of the glory of the next world to bring joy to the heart of the Christian.

What Have You Got?

Some years ago a poor man picked up a stone from a brook in North Carolina and took it home to hold his door open. Later on, a geologist who stopped by saw the lump at his door and recognized it as gold. It proved to be the biggest lump of gold ever found east of the Rockies! The man who found it had lived just as poorly after he found it as before.

You and I have a great treasure in our homes—our Bibles. Do we live as if we did not own them? Or are we using those Bibles in our personal devotional life? It is never sufficient to hear the Scriptures expounded

in church; we must personally pursue the reading and
study of them in our private lives.

always on the shelf

Two Kinds

There are two kinds of love for the Bible. One is
love in the abstract. It is something like the infatuation
of young people who are in love with love instead of
being in love with each other. It is sentimental and
very misleading. This kind of love for the Bible will
cause you to buy a nice copy and display it prom-
inently. It will have an honored place on the table or
shelf, but not in your daily life. It will be treasured, but
unknown; a charm to insure good fortune and make
you feel pious, but not a daily companion to insure
holiness and spiritual strength.

T and P

In contrast, there is true love for the Scriptures. A
friend of mine was called home to heaven. The family
showed her Bible which was well-marked and tear-
stained. Again and again by the tear stains were the
letters *T* and *P*, which stood for "tried and proved."
This person had had more heartache than most individuals, but her Christian walk and service could not
have been more exemplary. Her example came about
because of her devotion to her Lord and His Word. In
sorrow the Word had sustained her. In joy it had kept
her on course. In success it had disciplined her. The
words on the page had truly become God's Word to
her. And it was God's Word!

Since the Bible has the answers to life's deepest
and most urgent problems, we need to get the most
out of it. As we take time day by day to discover God's
message for us in our meditation on the Bible, we will

increasingly see things from God's perspective and new light will be shed on our opportunities.

There is a triad on reading the Bible that is loaded with meaning: "Read it to be wise, believe it to be safe, practice it to be holy."

Read It to Be Wise

President Herbert Hoover paid the Bible a tribute on this point: "There is no other book so various as the Bible, nor one so full of concentrated wisdom." The Bible instructs the mind.

Believe It to Be Safe

Paul the Apostle taught: "The holy Scriptures . . . are able to make thee wise unto salvation through faith which is in Christ Jesus" (2 Timothy 3:15). The Bible teaches the soul.

Live It to Be Holy

Abraham Lincoln found the Bible to be a guide for life. "I am profitably engaged in reading the Bible," he wrote. "Take all of this Book upon reason that you can, and the balance by faith, and you will live and die a better man." The Bible ties time and eternity together.

Dr. Carl G. Morlock, professor of clinical medicine and consultant in internal medicine at the world-famous Mayo Clinic in Rochester, Minnesota, states:

> I try to set aside some portion of each day for Bible reading and prayer. When, however, the press of work crowds out time that should be given to these matters, I find that my personal life suffers. The Bible is a secure guide for living in a world which seems to be evermore uncertain of what is best in human conduct.

The Bible should be read daily. God has so made us

that we need to replenish our bodies with food daily to remain physically healthy and active. In like manner, our souls and our spirits must be fed daily with the life-giving food of the Word of God if we are to be spiritually healthy.

Intellect...Emotions...Will

We daily read our Bibles, not because we have to read God's Word, but because we need to supply our daily spiritual need. We have *needs of the intellect*—our minds are the prime target of the devil. We have *needs in the emotional side* of our lives—anger, jealousy, and the like will yield to emotional control through the power of the Word and the Spirit. We have *needs regarding our will*—that part of our being that regulates choices is the will. We will not do the will of God until we learn what it is by our knowledge of His Word.

When the will is yielded daily, the mind and the emotions follow along in obedience. Our growth in grace can be measured by the growth of our love for daily Bible reading. Something is surely wrong when we lose our appetite for the Bread of Life.

Cod Liver Oil, Or...

Someone has named three stages of Bible study. The first is the cod liver oil stage. You take it like medicine. The second is the shredded wheat stage — dry yet nourishing. The third stage is peaches and cream. *w/ Holy Spirit*

Prayerful reading of the Bible will keep a love for the Scriptures aflame within us. The truth of the Word comes like a fire from God's heart to ours; its warmth warms us. The Word of God is the burning bush out of which comes the flame of fire.

When we approach God's Word with an attitude of prayer and worship, we no longer face it as a task. It need not be hard work. We need the approach of Mary, not Martha. Martha was "cumbered"—duty must be done. Mary sat at the feet of Jesus and drank in His words.

We must wash our garments in prayer to prepare ourselves to hear the Word of the Lord. Wait on the Lord to realize His presence. A few minutes spent quietly waiting on God are far more profitable than a longer time spent in frenzied hurry. The Holy Spirit will always bring some message to our hearts as we take time to ponder. Prayer and meditation are the means by which we assimilate into our spiritual system the Word which we read each day.

Tuck Away

It has been said that reading the Bible is good and studying it is better, but memorizing it is best of all. If you are ready to invest a little time and effort to accumulate something far more valuable than money, here is a way to begin. Simply stated, it is "tuck away a verse a day."

The Bible advocates Scripture memorization. The Psalmist declares: "Thy word have I hid in mine heart, that I might not sin against thee" (Psalm 119:11). The apostle Paul counsels: "Let the word of Christ dwell in you richly" (Colossians 3:16). And he also urges us to "take . . . the sword of the Spirit, which is the word of God" (Ephesians 6:17).

There are many benefits that come to us as we memorize Scripture. Some of the best may be seen under the following headings:

78

Victory

It is very significant that our Lord Jesus Christ, in the tremendous battle with Satan in the desert, used Scripture in each of the three temptations to defeat the devil. Again and again in my personal experience the Holy Spirit has come to my aid with a portion of the Word that I had committed to memory. Jesus promised the Holy Spirit will "bring all things to your remembrance" (John 14:26). If that Word has never lodged in our memory, how can He bring it to our remembrance? If the sinless Son of God used the sword of the Spirit in the hour of temptation, how much more we need to follow His example.

Comfort

In times of loneliness, illness, pain, or insomnia, there is great comfort in dwelling on the "exceeding great and precious promises" by which we are made "partakers of the divine nature" (2 Peter 1:4).

Many years ago I was sorely tried during a time of great doctrinal conflict which rocked an entire movement. As a young man elected to a responsible place of leadership in our Movement, the divisive struggle weighed heavily on me to the extent that I could feel it physically—I felt utterly exhausted through a series of events. Arriving home about 3 a.m. after a late meeting at a distant point, I found myself so spent I could not sleep. As I waited before God in prayer, He dropped a bit of Gilead's balm into my weary mind and spirit—"In quietness and in confidence shall be your strength" (Isaiah 30:15).

All problems were solved in my heart. Yes, the problems still existed, but they weren't mine to bear. God brought release and peace. It was a blessed payoff

of having committed the verse to memory years
before. The Holy Spirit knew when to meet my need
by quickening my memory.

Guidance

Life seems to be made up of a succession of deci-
sions. Some days it not only rains, it also pours—
challenge heaps on another. Here is where God's
Word helps us. The Word is a "lamp unto my feet, and
a light unto my path.... The entrance of thy words
giveth light; it giveth understanding unto the simple"
(Psalm 119:105, 130). "I will instruct thee and teach
thee in the way which thou shalt go: I will guide thee
with mine eye" (Psalm 32:8). "And thine ears shall
hear a word behind thee, saying, This is the way, walk
ye in it" (Isaiah 30:21). How blessed when the Spirit
brings truth to our memory when we are in need of
guidance.

Meditation

Among the many commendable things said of the
man in Psalm 1 is: "His delight is in the law of the Lord;
and in his law doth he meditate day and night" (v. 2).
What blessing has come to me as I have meditated on
the Word while traveling, waiting for an appointment,
or just pausing to think on the Lord. We talk about "40
winks" for physical refreshing. We also need the "40
winks" of meditation for a spiritual pickup.

Witness

The Christian who is best equipped to lead others
to the Saviour is the one who knows the Word. To be
able to wield the sword of the Spirit—to use appro-

priate Scripture as you are led by the Spirit—is a rewarding experience. The same can be said with regard to sharing a word with a fellow Christian who has a spiritual, physical, or temporal need.

Memorizing God's Word provides its own defense against the obstacles we face. It will supply us with the resources we need for victorious Christian living (2 Timothy 3:16, 17). Now to do it. Decide you are going to learn Scripture. Pray about it. Ask God's help. Get started. Keep a packet of verses or portions with you. Keep it on your desk, in your lunch bucket, or over the kitchen sink. Choose a plan. Keep at it. The rewards are tremendous.

9

Devotional and Study Helps

Devotional thoughts should find a solid foundation in the Scriptures. A good study Bible is important. Get one with readable print. To encourage people to read the Bible, and then lead them to buy Bibles with small print that makes reading laborious, is self-defeating.

The Holy Spirit has graciously used choice servants to prepare tools to aid us in our devotional life. These are found in reference materials in various Bibles and in many other study helps.

Over 500 translations of the English Bible in whole or in part have been published since the King James Version in 1611; the majority being translated in recent decades. It is a startling fact that at this hour English-speaking people have the choice of more important new versions than at any other time in history.

Translations and Paraphrases

There is a difference between a translation and a paraphrase. A translation is the "rendering from one language to another." A paraphrase is the restatement of a text already translated, giving the meaning in another form. Generally the work of one man, a paraphrase allows for latitude and more freedom of expression. Sometimes the translator becomes an interpreter in a paraphrase.

Reference Bibles

Reference Bibles include: *Thompson's Chain Reference Bible*, the *Dickson Analytical Edition*, the *Scofield Reference Bible*, *The Ryrie Study Bible*, the *Holman Study Bible*, the *New Oxford Reference Bible*, *The Englishman's Bible* by Newberry, *The Emphasized Bible* by Rotherham, and *The Chronological Bible*.

Several of these Bibles offer extensive materials such as a dictionary, concordance, topical study, chronology, harmony of the Gospels, maps, charts, outlines, etc. Always remember that interpretive footnotes are subject to judgment. They are not the Bible.

While modern-language Bibles are widely used, you will want to own a King James Version which is still the most widely used translation. The *New King James Bible* conforms to the thought flow of the 1611 version, but eliminates the Elizabethan pronouns (*thee, thou, thy, thine, ye*) and verb endings (*eth* and *est*, such as loveth, doest, etc.).

Contemporary Translations

Great benefit comes from the contemporary translations. The *New International Version* (NIV) is gaining rapid recognition as a faithful translation and a literary masterpiece that "sounds like the Bible." The *New American Standard Bible* (NASB) is a conservative revision that has much to commend it. The *New English Bible* has some passages where apparently translation is combined with interpretation. *Today's English Version* (TEV), popularly known as *Good News for Modern Man*, is easy to read, giving it rather wide appeal.

The Living Bible is the most popular paraphrase. No doubt its use of colloquialisms and contemporary language has made it appealing. *Phillips* is a colorful, vigorous paraphrase of contemporary idiom with dignity.

The Amplified Bible and *Wuest's Expanded Translation* are helpful interpretive translations. Helpful insights can be gained from *Weymouth, Moffatt, Goodspeed, Montgomery, Williams, Way, Beck,* and *Berkeley.* Watch for liberal theology in *Goodspeed* and *Moffatt. Worrell's* is an excellent translation.

Several parallel translations are now on the market, such as *The New Testament From 26 Translations, The Six Version Parallel New Testament,* and *The New Testament in Four Versions.*

Bible-Reading Guides

Daily Bible-reading guides are very helpful to many Christians. They keep us on course as to faithfulness in reading and help us to cover the entire Bible. The normal tendency is to give prominence to those portions that have become special to us and to neglect the passages that are more difficult to understand. Just as a growing child and a healthy adult must eat a well-balanced diet, Christians must also have a balanced diet from God's Word.

The Gospel Publishing House in Springfield, Missouri, offers several Bible-reading plans. "The Bible in a Year" takes you through the Bible in a year. "Through the Bible This Year" is a day-by-day chronological guide presenting the order in which events took place. "Scriptures To Live By" keeps its selections to a different topic each week. "Great Chapters" increases your knowledge of the Word as you progress through the great chapters of the Bible, a chapter a day.

Devotional Books

For many years the Gospel Publishing House has published *God's Word for Today.* Each quarterly issue has a daily devotional commentary on a given passage of Scripture. Several other devotional books, such as *Streams in the Desert,* are also available.

Next to the Bible—A Concordance

Now a word about selecting Bible study helps. Next to a good cross-referenced Bible the most important tool for Bible study is, in my opinion, a complete concordance to the Scriptures. A concordance provides immediate access to any verse of the Bible, even if you only remember a part of it. Efforts are just under way to develop concordances for translations other than the King James. A good concordance will enable you to discover the precise meaning of a word or phrase as you examine the various passages where the word occurs. This will be especially true as you trace the Hebrew and Greek words that are translated by the same English word.

Leading concordances are Young's *Analytical Concordance to the Bible,* Strong's *Exhaustive Concordance of the Bible,* Cruden's *Complete Concordance,* and *The Zondervan Expanded Concordance.* The last one lists about 250,000 key Biblical words for seven modern versions (*Berkeley, American Standard, Amplified, New English, New Scofield, Phillips, Revised Standard*) as well as the King James.

Get a Good Bible Dictionary

Another valuable tool is a good Bible dictionary; it is a bargain at any price. You are cheating yourself if you don't have one available. Why? It will help you identify any person, place, or thing you read about but don't understand. Just as a good dictionary should be in every home, every Bible reader should have a Bible dictionary. A carpenter without a hammer and saw is like a student without a dictionary.

Two kinds of Bible dictionaries are available—the single-volume and multiple-volume. The latter type gives a more in-depth treatment of the subjects listed. Among the better known works are *The New Bible Dictionary* by Douglas, *Unger's Bible Dictionary, Davis Dictionary of the Bible,* and *Smith's Bible Dictionary.* For more extensive help there are the five-volume *Zondervan Pictorial Encyclopedia of the Bible* by Tenney, *The International Standard Bible Encyclopedia* in five volumes, the four-volume *Dictionary of the Bible* by Smith, and the two-volume *Wycliffe Bible Encyclopedia.*

Other Aids

The history and geography of the Bible are made vivid through the help of a Bible atlas. Geography, geology, and archaeology come alive through this tool. To name a few, I mention *Baker's Bible Atlas,* the *Oxford Bible Atlas,* the *MacMillan Bible Atlas,* and *The Land of Israel* by Stewart.

A Bible handbook (such as *Halley's, Unger's, Angus-Green's* or the *Handbook to the Bible*), is also a useful tool although it may duplicate information in other types of books. It could be a substitute for those who do not wish to invest in a number of books.

Two other books should be mentioned: *Nave's Top-*

ical Bible and *Torrey's Topical Textbook.* These aids arrange subjects in topical fashion.

Brief mention can be made of commentaries. As implied by its name, a Bible commentary comments on Scripture, passage by passage and verse by verse, with the purpose of interpreting meaning. Although now over 300 years old, Matthew Henry's comments are still the standard for a concise devotional commentary.

A number of Bible study tools have been named and specific titles have been mentioned, but this list is limited and does not necessarily name the best book in a given field. Personal preferences will vary. This is only an attempt to assist those who are interested in aids for Bible study.

Now, a word of caution. The Bible must be read and studied independently of all other aids. Christians today have more helpful books for Bible study than Christians of any previous time. We need to use these tools—Bible dictionaries, atlases, annotated Bibles, handbooks, commentaries—with enthusiasm and diligence. The harvest of the labors of able evangelical scholars will bless your life. But keep the Bible central! And remember ultimate learning comes through the illumination of the Holy Spirit!

10

Praise and Worship

There was a billboard, common to the corn and hog country of our nation, advertising pig starter. A row of little pigs were gulping the starter from a trough—that is, all but one. This little fellow didn't have his head in the trough; he was looking up, head cocked, watching every vehicle going by as though the traffic had caught his attention. He wasn't too busy to look up from the trough.

The billboard grabbed the attention of a preacher as he went by. He kept mulling it over as he drove on. What made one pig look up from the trough?

The Holy Spirit brought the application to his mind. It was Thanksgiving time. His seasonal sermon was titled, "Have You Looked up From the Trough Lately?"

Even More About Praise

We talk about prayer a great deal. But the Psalms talk about praise even more. This Book, also called the Psalter, with 150 chapters, is properly called the "Book of Praises." The original Hebrew title is a work meaning "praises." In the Greek language the word *psalm* means "songs." The Book of Psalms is a collection of 150 different songs, largely songs of praise. It is an inspired hymnbook setting forth the thoughts, feelings, and aspirations of the people of God in every conceivable circumstance. The innermost thoughts of men are shared, but through it all the dominant chord of praise to God is sounded.

But it is not in the Psalms alone that we read of praise. Throughout the Bible God is the object of praise. His whole creation praises Him, from the angels of heaven (Psalm 103:20; Revelation 5:11, 12) to all forms of existence, from animal life to the sun, moon, and stars (Psalms 19:1-4; 148; Revelation 5:13, 14).

Over 600 Times

Check a good concordance and you'll find that *praise, praising,* and *praises* are mentioned over 350 times in the Bible. The word *praise* or the word *rejoice* in its various forms appears over 600 times. We are commanded to "sing praise" more than 50 times; and the expression "praise ye the Lord," which is actually a translation of the word *hallelujah,* is found more than 25 times.

A Command With Purpose

The Bible does not hint several hundred times that it might be good to praise the Lord; it commands us. Praise is not optional; it is a binding obligation. But while the Bible commands us to be praiseful and thankful ("this is the will of God in Christ Jesus concerning you"), God's commands are never given without purpose. While praise is due the name and character of God, there is another reason for us to praise Him. We praise Him for His worthiness and recognize our unworthiness.

89

Praising results in our good as well as God's honor. When we exalt Him, the bad, the dark, and the ugly in us disappear). The lovely, the gracious, and the good take over. Through praise we open the door for the Spirit to enter and work to make us Christlike. Praising blesses the praiser; all the while giving the praised One the homage due Him.

Out of a Babe's Mouth

Jesus quoted Psalm 8:2 when He said: "Out of the mouth of babes and sucklings thou hast perfected praise" (Matthew 21:16). As you think of the innocency of babies, you will begin to realize why the Lord found in them perfected praise. Their minds are not polluted with the filth of this world. Their mouths have not been defiled with foul speech and the dregs of evil habits. Their ears are not attentive to evil speaking, falsehoods, gossip, criticism, and backbiting. Their eyes have never looked on evil, lustful scenes, obscene literature, and trashy filth. Virtue is wrapped up in those innocent bundles.

God can cleanse and make us free from sin and its power. We must guard our lives so we do not become self-centered and self-seeking. As sweet and bitter water do not come from the same source, neither do "perfected praise" and "foul speech" proceed from the same source.

> Out of the same mouth proceedeth blessing and cursing. My brethren, these things ought not so to be. Does a fountain send forth at the same place sweet water and bitter? (James 3:10, 11).

Don't expect God to honor your hypocrisy as you give praise to Him in the church service and then live

90

and speak the opposite away from the church. To have perfected praise, you must serve God with your whole heart. Practice what the Psalmist said: "I will bless the Lord at all times: his praise shall continually be in my mouth" (Psalm 34:1).

Five Books

The Book of Psalms is composed of five sections. Each section or book closes with a doxology. Book I (Psalms 1-41) ends with this praise: "Blessed be the Lord God of Israel from everlasting and to everlasting. Amen, and Amen." Book II (Psalms 42-72) concludes with: "Blessed be the Lord God . . . and blessed be his glorious name for ever: and let the whole earth be filled with his glory. Amen, and Amen."

Book III (Psalms 73-89) closes with: "Blessed be the Lord forevermore. Amen, and Amen." And Book IV (Psalms 90-106) ends with: "Blessed be the Lord God of Israel from everlasting to everlasting: and let all the people say, Amen. Praise ye the Lord." This last expression, "Praise ye the Lord," is often translated *Hallelujah*.

Book V (Psalms 107-150) climaxes with six psalms (145-150) of praise, closing with: "Let every thing that hath breath praise the Lord. Praise ye the Lord [Hallelujah]." These six psalms are called David's Psalm of Praise.

In introducing David's Psalm of Praise, the Psalmist almost exhausts the vocabulary of terms for praise. Look at them as they appear in Psalm 145.

Extol

Extol (v. 1) means *to lift up, to exalt with praises, celebrate*. The Hebrew word is *rum*. New Testament passages that reflect this word are: "Glory to God in the highest" (Luke 2:14); and, "Hosanna in the highest" (Matthew 21:9). Note also Psalm 149:6: "Let the high praises of God be in their mouth."

Bless

Bless (vv. 1, 2, 10, 21) means to worship on bended knee in humble acknowledgment of God's mercies. The Hebrew word is *barak* and comes from a root which means to "kneel down." God blesses us, and we are to bless Him.

Praise

Praise (vv. 2, 3), translated from the Hebrew word *halal*, means "to be clear, to be brilliant." When we praise God, we make His name to shine. "Make his praise glorious" (Psalm 66:2).

Praise (v. 4), translated from the Hebrew word *shabach*, means "to gratify." Can't you imagine how gratifying to God must be the praises of His people?

Praise (v. 10), from the Hebrew word *yadah*, means "to cast forth as stones or words, to throw out with the hand." It is from this word that the name *Judah* is derived (Genesis 29:35). Leah said, "Now will I praise the Lord: therefore, she called his name Judah." Jacob referred to this when he gave his dying blessing— "Judah, thou art he whom thy brethren shall praise" (Genesis 49:8).

Declare

Declare (v. 4), from the Hebrew word *nagad*, means "to bring to light, show, tell, declare, profess openly, proclaim, celebrate with praise." Jubilant declarations!

Speak

Speak (v. 21), from the Hebrew *dabar,* is translated "talk" in verse 11 and is used of inspired utterance giving praise to God.

Speak (vv. 6, 11), from the Hebrew *amar,* means "to speak" or "say," the ordinary word for conversation—everyday speech, daily conversation filled with praise.

A Gushing Spring

Abundantly utter (v. 7), from the Hebrew *naba,* means "to bubble forth" or "gush out as waters from a spring." It is translated "pour out" in Proverbs 1:23. Praise is a gushing spring of fervent expressions of adoration.

Sound It Out

Sing (v. 7) is from the Hebrew *ranan.* Among its meanings is "to emit a tremulous and stridulous sound," "to trill the voice," "to shout for joy." So full that you shout with pure delight and leap with gladness!

To Know and Make Known

Make known (v. 12), from the Hebrew *yada,* means "to see or perceive," "to know by personal experience," "to discover; then to make known to someone else."

Our Chief End

The oft-quoted catechism asks the question, "What is the chief end of man?" And the answer is, "The chief end of man is to glorify God and enjoy Him forever." In other words, you can define your life as committed to glorifying God.

An excellent way to glorify God is to praise Him.
"Whoso offereth praise glorifieth me" (Psalm 50:23).
"I will praise thee, Oh Lord, my God, with all my
heart: and I will glorify thy name for evermore" (Psalm
86:12). "It is a good thing to give thanks unto the Lord,
and to sing praises unto thy name, O Most High"
(Psalm 92:1).

We glorify God in praise as we recite His attributes.
Read about the life of David in the Psalms. Troubles
would beset him, and he would start to pour out his
heart. Suddenly he would stop and begin to recite
God's character and qualities. He would conclude the
psalm with a tremendous lift: "God, You're great. I'm
excited about what You are going to do!"

We glorify God when we recall His works. Jeremiah,
the weeping prophet, presents five lamentations in
the Book bearing that name. In recalling all of the
sorrows, he moans, "My soul hath them still in remembrance, and is humbled in me" (Lamentations
3:20). But then he finds hope and courage as he recalls
God's works!

> This I recall to my mind, therefore have I hope. It is of
> the Lord's mercies that we are not consumed, because his
> compassions fail not. They are new every morning: great
> is thy faithfulness (vv. 21-23).

We glorify God when we give Him thanks. Nine of the
ten lepers who were healed by the Lord never returned to say, "Thank you." Only one "turned back
and . . . glorified God" (Luke 17:11-19).

Drinking at Joel's Place

Praise is attractive. "Praise is comely" (Psalm 33:1)
literally means praise is attractive. The Apostolic

94

Church was marked by much praising. The writer of Acts describes those early Christians as, "Praising God, and having favor with all the people" (Acts 2:47). They had been drinking at "Joel's place" and were spiritually intoxicated.

Worship—Ministry to the Lord

"Worthy is the Lamb...to receive" (Revelation 5:12). "As they ministered to the Lord" (Acts 13:2). The expression *ministry to the Lord*, as used here, does not refer to ministry as being done unto the Lord. It is, rather, an expression synonymous with the word *worship*.

What Is Ministry to the Lord?

The Revelation states, "Worthy is the Lamb...to *receive*." Do we not place the emphasis here all too seldom? Again and again we come to our Lord that we might receive from Him. And when we do come to Him with an expression of grateful praise, is it not for what He does for us? This is well and good. But how much time do we spend in adoration of Him for who He is rather than for what He has done? This latter should not be left undone, but do you not think He also craves expression of our love for who He is?

11

Results in Ourselves

Ralph Keiper tells of taking a Roman Catholic friend to St. Patrick's Cathedral while on a tour of New York City. During their visit at the cathedral, his friend came to the altar of the saint whose name he had taken at baptism.

While Keiper waited, the friend lit a candle, knelt, said a prayer, and put his coin in the appropriate slot. Then as they continued their walk, Keiper noticed the next altar was in total darkness. Walking closer, they noted that a sign on it read: "Do not worship at this altar; it is out of order." He went on to say after his momentary surprise, "Aren't you lucky that your saint was in order?"

Our bodies are the temples of the Holy Spirit:

> Do you not know that your body is the temple—the very sanctuary—of the Holy Spirit Who lives within you, Whom you have received [as a Gift] from God? You are not your own, You were bought for a price—purchased with a preciousness and paid for, made His own. So then, honor God and bring glory to Him in your body (1 Corinthians 6:19, 20, *The Amplified Bible*).

The word translated "temple" could be rendered "shrine." There are two words in the Greek for temple: *hieron*, which means the entire building, es-

96

pecially the nave of a cathedral; and *naos*, which means the "shrine," where the image of the god resides in pagan religion.

Christians are the *naos*, the shrine, of the Holy Spirit. If we do not maintain our devotional life, our shrine will be out of order. Can others see an "out of order" sign on your temple?

A Special Dimension

The blessings of a devotional life are beyond enumeration. The full range of prayer, from worship to intercession, brings us into contact with God. The balancing power of the Word is always needed. In his devotional life, a Pentecostal Christian has the dimensions of worshiping and praying with a tongue other than the one he has learned (Acts 2:4; 10:45-47; 19:6). Supernatural equipment is given to believers to do the work of God (1 Corinthians 12).

The gift of prophecy (1 Corinthians 12:10) is for speaking to men supernaturally (1 Corinthians 14:3). The latter verse also tells us the gift is given for "edification, and exhortation, and comfort" and that believers "may learn" (v. 31). There is also the gift of tongues. In tongues men speak to God supernaturally (1 Corinthians 14:2); in prophecy God speaks to men supernaturally.

Taken alone, tongues is for private prayer and worship; with its sister gift of interpretation, it becomes the means of edifying the church (1 Corinthians 14:5, 14, 15, 28). The interpretation can be petition, praise, or thanksgiving. The gift is not for personal guidance or for the spread of the gospel. Prophecy is shown to be greater than tongues unless tongues is accompanied by interpretation (1 Corin-

97

thians 14:23-25). In essence, tongues with interpretation is equivalent to prophecy.

The Gifts and the Word

These gifts are for "edification, and exhortation, and comfort." The words spoken in these manifestations are subject to being judged (1 Corinthians 14:29). On the other hand, the written Word is the standard by which all is judged. That Word is "profitable for doctrine, for reproof, for correction, for instruction in righteousness" (2 Timothy 3:16).

In other words, the Pentecostal believer has a wonderful dimension in his devotional life of worshiping and praying in other tongues. But that manifestation is subject to the Word. The Word is the standard by which all is to be measured.

Devotional life, both group and individual, is very important and meaningful to a Pentecostal Christian. The infilling of the Spirit is not an end in itself, but only the entrance into a deeper, more joyful, and victorious life in the Spirit.

Dennis and Rita Bennett, in their book *The Holy Spirit and You* (Plainfield, NJ: Logos International, 1971), state:

> As a Christian baptized in the Holy Spirit, you will find the Bible speaking to you all the way through, even though you do not always understand the background of what you are reading. This is the most important use of the Scriptures, to let the Holy Spirit speak to you . . . .
> Intellectual understanding and training in the faith are important, but the most important ministry of the Bible to you will be *inspiration*. You need to let God speak to you personally through His Word. The Christian life must be an interplay of *experience* and *truth* (pp. 194-207).

Life Changing

Devotional life balanced with prayer and the Word will bring life-changing experiences. Prayer and the Word create within us a sense of our absolute dependence on God; not merely for our salvation from sin or our material good, but for our continuance in Him. Without a devotional life we would not realize, as we should, our utter dependence on the Almighty. A proper sense of dependence produces in us a proper humility before God, and right emotions of gratitude and love to Him.

By prayer we get to know God. We come with all of our sorrows and failures, aspirations and disappointments. By this means God brings us face to face with Him and ourselves as we are. Because we must abandon sin or be defeated, we come with a single eye. Prayer becomes a means of self-discovery and purification.

Lead in Your Pitcher?

If there is a piece of lead weighing a pound in the bottom of a pitcher, you could pump all the water in the Atlantic Ocean into that pitcher, but you couldn't fill it until you took the lead out. A devotional life will remove the "lead" so our pitcher can be filled.

The Spiritual Lifeline

Communication with God is our spiritual lifeline. On our faithfulness in prayer and reading the Word, depend our strength, our overcoming grace, and our fruitful living. "Prayer is the Christian's native air." Through communion the Spirit of God anoints us with the life of God.

Communion with God leads to the discovery of the excellence of God's character. Your soul is transformed by beholding God. The devotional life develops holiness and Christlikeness. Holiness is conformity to Christ, a habit of your mind setting Christ before your eyes, and a continuing walk with Him resulting in a growing intimacy with Him. Someone has called a life of rich devotion a building up "into a recollected consciousness of God."

Keys to the Pantry

A poor widow lived alone in the country. She was asked how she was getting along at a time when conditions in general were most difficult. Her response was great: "I do very well. I get more of one verse of the Bible now than of it ever before. God has handed me the keys to the pantry door and bid me to take my fill."

A devotional life will bring you inner strength and spiritual growth. It will be a deterrent to sin and develop power in you to resist temptation and the evil that is everywhere about you.

It Pays to Wait

Isaiah 40:28-31 directs us to the source of spiritual victory:

> But they that wait upon the Lord shall renew their strength; they shall mount up with wings as eagles; they shall run, and not be weary; and they shall walk, and not faint (v. 31).

God has promised "power to the faint; and to them that have no might he increaseth strength." Little wonder that we become tired and worn out. Even

100

youths shall be exhausted, and young men all give up. There is, however, a promise of renewed strength. But that promise rests on a condition—"wait upon the Lord." Waiting implies expectancy. And it also implies service. Waiting is not an idle or impassive thing; there is active attention to whatever the Master's command may be.

Several important lessons regarding the need for and the blessings of a devotional life are found in this passage from Isaiah. First, natural strength is not sufficient. And, second, those that wait upon the Lord shall "renew their strength." As sleep refreshes the tired body, so waiting on God strengthens the soul. Without sleep physical strength wanes; without the rest found in regularly waiting on God spiritual strength diminishes.

In Need of Therapy?

Waiting on the Lord provides the therapy so desperately needed in this jet age with its jangled nerves and frayed relationships. A well-known medical doctor writing in the *Reader's Digest* expressed his firm belief in prayer as a definite means of strengthening the body and the mind, and of soothing tired nerves. We present our weaknesses and God gives us strength.

The Greeks had a legend of the earthborn Antaeus who could not be overcome by the ordinary process of knocking him down. Every time he touched the earth he revived. The Christian, however, reverses that order. Every time he is knocked down he revives because he is heaven-born.

There are natural distinctions among people. Some individuals are naturally courageous and strong;

others are timid and fearful. The gospel refuses to recognize natural weakness as final, but proclaims its power to make believers brave and strong. Your strength will be renewed day after day, and you can work without wearing out.

When Christians wait on the Lord, they will be as eagles that can fly to the heights, as runners who do not become weary, and as walkers who do not faint. They will fly, run, and walk. Most of us would have reversed the order—walk, run, and climax with flying. Why did the Lord use the order given in Scripture? Possibly to teach us that steady perseverance, plodding on, is more remarkable than soaring.

How to Kill Rats

"They shall mount up with wings as eagles." An aviator flying low over the desert heard a gnawing sound in a section of his plane. He recognized the sound and immediately nosed his plane up and up and up. Finally the gnawing stopped. After landing the plane, he checked the area where he had heard the gnawing. Sure enough, he found a large desert rat now cold and dead. If the rat had kept gnawing there could have been a wreck, but the aviator knew the secret—attaining high altitude.

Life With Wings

Waiting on God will bring you to the place of seeking "those things which are above, where Christ sitteth on the right hand of God" and setting "your affection on things above, not on things on the earth" (Colossians 3:1, 2).

The life with wings will be marked by buoyancy.

102

There is a lift that carries us above our circumstances. We can ride the currents and rise higher. We do not need to go around moaning or grumbling "under the circumstances." Divine provision has been made for us to rise above circumstances.

The life with wings will give us heavenly-mindedness. Our sights will be on the rich treasures and joys of heaven. Heaven will fill our thoughts. Earth's standards are beggarly—low affections, low thinking, low dealing. Paul always kept obedience to the heavenly vision in focus (Acts 26:19).

The life with wings will give us the far look. Correct perspective comes through getting God's viewpoint as you soar to His observation platform and view the surroundings below through His telescope.

Getting Your Second Wind

"They shall run and not be weary." In running special demands are placed on the body. From the time I was a boy I have done a lot of running. I know what it is to get my "second wind." They that wait upon the Lord know what it is to get their "second wind" spiritually.

The experience of getting my "second wind" when running comes when I feel too exhausted to go on. The natural inclination would be to quit, but then there comes a sudden rush of new energy. The lungs draw breath evenly, adrenaline flows, and my tired body takes on new strength. From somewhere deep within I draw on a new source of endurance.

No Shortcut for Winning

The runner does not wait until the day of the race to train. His training starts long before. And more than wind sprints and mile after mile of conditioning is involved. Diet, rest, proper exercise, and warm-ups are important. My son's high school track coach won 17 state championships in 21 years in cross-country running. One of his secrets of success with the hundreds of boys he trained was his attention to details and demand for discipline in training.

If you as a Christian are to have the reserve strength for the inevitable crises that come in the race of life, you must be careful to obey the training rules laid down by the great Trainer, the Lord Jesus Christ. And the basic rule is to wait upon the Lord. Great men were always good "runners"—ready to obey and act (Genesis 18:2; 1 Samuel 3:5; 1 Kings 18:46; 19:20; Luke 19:4; Acts 14:14). The Psalmist has a good word for us—"I will run the way of thy commandments, when thou shalt enlarge my heart" (Psalm 119:32).

Life Has a Lotta Ordinariness

"They shall walk and not faint." Why are these words last in the triad—flying, running, and now walking? Is it not because everyday life consists of plodding through a very ordinary existence? Walking is moving at an ordinary rate of speed. Life is made up of ordinary things, for the most part. There are mountain peaks of thrilling adventures, but in general we live life in the vale of ordinariness.

There is no standing still in life. "Every man walketh" (Psalm 39:6). Walking speaks of progress. We are always caught up with the spectacular; very seldom with the routine. We need to be aware that fidgeting and restless moving around are not spiritual activity. Successes are largely the result of determination in the routine.

Did You Ever Describe Walking?

Walking is an interesting procedure. It's a rapid vibration between points of weight placement resulting in a smooth, even course. We put all our weight on one foot, then on the other, with such a rapid shift that there is no vibration. We don't walk on just one foot, nor with both feet tied together. When we walk, we don't put all our weight on both feet at the same time.

Notice these things about walking:

1. Walking takes place on the ground.

2. Walking is done in the open. We don't walk in a closet.

3. Walking is a steady and graceful means of motion, putting one foot ahead of another.

4. Walking gets you to your destination.

Walking with God is the highest privilege of a Christian. Walking with God means communion with God, submission to His will, confidence in His love, and delight in the Lord himself. *Motion* is implied. Lethargy, laziness, and sloth are impossible if you really walk. *Direction* is implied. You are not to wander, but to walk toward a destination. The prophet Amos raised an interesting question, "Can two walk together, except they be agreed?" (Amos 3:3). God leads the way and sets the pace. We must agree with His plan and purpose.

Known by Your Walk

Even from a distance, we often recognize a friend by the way he walks. I know the footsteps of my wife, even though she hasn't yet appeared in sight. Our years of living together have tuned my ears to the sound of her step.

These Walked With God

The Bible tells us of three men who walked with God—Enoch (Genesis 5:24), Noah (Genesis 6:9), and Abraham (Genesis 17:1).

"Enoch walked with God." In four simple words we have the picture of one of God's greats. For over 300 years in the midst of the cares and anxieties of family life, the joys and sorrows, and the gains and losses of all of life, Enoch walked with God. While others lived selfishly and carelessly without God, Enoch walked with the Lord without faltering.

To walk with God is to have God's best. "No good will he withhold from them that walk uprightly" (Psalm 84:11). Think of the two sad-faced and sad-hearted disciples on their way to Emmaus. Theirs was a unique privilege. They heard the Great Teacher open the Scriptures to them and their hearts burned within them. What great lessons they learned in an hour or two with their risen Lord. What treasures await us as we spend a lifetime in hallowed intimacy with Him.

12

Ever Get in a Fog?

A friend lives in a beautiful setting on the edge of a lake in the mountains. The view from his home is breathtaking. When the air is clear, the mountains stand in sharp outline—an artist's paradise.

At times a fog settles on the lake. There is a haze that obliterates the mountains; you can't see them. But my friend has never doubted that the mountains are there. He has seen them when the horizon is clear.

That's the parable of our spiritual lives. Sometimes you see clearly. At other times you may feel that you are in a "fog." But regardless of the haze that seems to engulf you, you can have confidence in God.

> And this is the confidence that we have in him, that, if we ask any thing according to his will, he heareth us: and if we know that he hear us, whatsoever we ask, we know that we have the petitions that we desired of him (1 John 5:14, 15).

We'll Make It for You

Jesus made a great statement in John 15:7: "If ye abide in me, and my words abide in you, ye shall ask what ye will, and it shall be done unto you." The word for "done" is sometimes used for "create." God will create something out of nothing to answer the prayers

107

of His children who receive His Word and abide in His fellowship. The late P. C. Nelson, a great Bible scholar, said: "Jesus in essence was saying, 'If we don't have it in heaven, we will make it for you.' " By abiding in Him you get to know Him and learn to exercise faith.

Through communion the Holy Spirit anoints us with the life of God. Our prayer life—our communion, our waiting on God, our meditation—is the digestive system of the mind. By it, truth is turned into spiritual nourishment. Fail to let your thoughts feed on God's truth, and you will never be "like a tree planted by the rivers of water" (Psalm 1:3). In communion you take on the nature of God.

Grow at Both Ends

If you are to be like a tree, you must grow at both ends. A strong tree trunk reaches heavenward with branches furnishing beauty and shade. But there is no such development unless there is growth at the other end. There must be a good root system. All the sap— the life of the tree—flows upward from the unseen roots. You must reach down into the soil of God's truth to gain the needed nutrients for spiritual growth. Your spiritual strength and fruit depend on your ability to absorb the elements of God's provision through communion with the Lord and His life-giving Word. The "blessed" man of Psalm 1 is the one who meditates "day and night" on God's Word. What do you think upon? Answer that question, and you will describe the kind of a person you are.

Alterations Done Here

Prayer alters me. Prayer alters others. Prayer alters circumstances through me. Yes, prayer is very real.

Prayer is also mysterious. But all of us use things every day that are beyond our ability to explain. Do you understand electricity? Can you fully explain, or even understand, its nature? What a mysterious and wonderful fact that prayer alters us and things. In this sophisticated scientific age, prayer still works to bring about changes for God's glory and our good.

Con Fides

Let us turn our attention again to John's statement regarding our confidence in God (1 John 5:14, 15). Our English word for confidence comes from the Latin *con fides*, which connotes the sharing of faith between two persons. An intimate term, it signifies a closeness of fellowship in which troubles are made known, heartaches are shared, and burdens are unloaded. How do we have this fellowship—this confidence—with and in God?

Your confidence in God has to be based on two great facts: (1) the statements of God's Word, and (2) the death of Christ on the cross. The Cross is your eternal guarantee and your assurance that God will provide for you. "He that spared not his own Son, but delivered him up for us all, how shall he not with him also freely give us all things?" (Romans 8:32). For this reason you have every right to "come boldly unto the throne of grace, that [you] may obtain mercy, and find grace to help in time of need" (Hebrews 4:16).

Have You Felt God's Muscle?

Every boy likes to feel his dad's muscle. Have you felt the "muscle" of the Almighty? When you pray, you take hold of God. To take hold of God, you must take hold of His strength and His promises. Christ

109

crucified is stated to be the power of God and the wisdom of God. You lay hold of God's strength when you, with a believing heart, take hold of Jesus as the only and all-sufficient One. The Lord has in His love and grace hedged himself on every side by His infallible declarations and promises. And He has placed an obligation on you as His child to hold Him to His promises.

Added to this are the two absorbing passions of the Holy Spirit—to Christ first and then to His church. The Spirit comes to glorify Christ and not himself. He comes to guide the Church. Someone has said the Spirit is the Divine Innkeeper in whose care the Good Samaritan has left us.

The $64 Question

Where does the fault lie? If you are a child of God, and prayer is your privilege, and Jesus has promised to do anything for you, how come your prayers are not answered? Isn't God's Word true? Is God at fault? Are you to blame? Why are the heavens as brass? Why are answers not forthcoming?

Unanswered prayer is a perennial problem. The promises seem to be so broad and so positive. Most Christians have at some point had the experience of praying very urgently and definitely about something only to find that their prayer was seemingly unanswered.

Disappointment, Delay, and Denial

You may have heard that our disappointments are God's appointments; God's delays are not His denials. Delay, with its apparent shattering of all hope, can be a discipline to the person who would serve the

110

Lord. This discipline was vital in the life of Abraham who waited for decades for the promised son, in Joseph's years in Egypt as a victim of cruel circumstances, in Moses' lonely years in the desert, and in David's fleeing from Saul though he had been anointed king. Little wonder that David cried, "I am forgotten as a dead man out of mind: I am like a broken vessel" (Psalm 31:12).

The Urgent or the Important

A man and his two sisters faced an emergency, a matter of life and death. They prayed, but divine help seemingly arrived too late. The brother died. Mary and Martha were the sisters and Lazarus was the brother (John 11). Why didn't Jesus rush to Bethany immediately upon receiving word of Lazarus' illness? Didn't He love them? Where was His concern? Finally He went to Bethany, arriving 4 days after Lazarus' death. The "urgent" was to rush to Bethany to heal Lazarus; the "important" was to raise him from the dead. Jesus' delay was not due to indifference. He never delays because He does not care. A delayed answer may mean God's solution to our problem is better than our own.

George Muller, the outstanding man of prayer and faith, testified:

> I have myself had to wait a long time to get certain blessings. In many instances the answer has come instantaneously. In other things I had to wait ten years, fifteen, twenty years and upward; yet invariably at the last the answer has come (*Moody Monthly,* September 1970).

No less a man than the apostle Paul could write from experience about an unanswered prayer. He draws aside the veil and lets us gaze on his inner heart and experience (2 Corinthians 12:7-9). Three times Paul asked for deliverance from his thorn in the flesh. God's answer was, "No, My grace is sufficient for you."

No doubt some may say of Paul, "Oh, it was easy for him, with his experience, his knowledge, and his understanding." But Paul was just as human as you and I. Three words can be used to summarize Paul's experience: *frustration*—the painful thorn; *revelation*—"My grace is sufficient"; *transformation*—"Most gladly therefore will I rather glory in my infirmities, that the power of Christ may rest upon me."

Someone has well said that God *always lightens the burden* or *strengthens the back*. Most prayer requests seek to have God lighten the burden. God at times chooses to strengthen the back. Trials can be capital on which we can draw dividends. Don't forget that wind-blown, storm-tossed trees produce the most beautifully grained wood.

The Whatsoever of Prayer

"And whatsoever we ask, we receive of him, because we keep his commandments, and do those things that are pleasing in his sight" (1 John 3:22). God's "whatsoever" is subject to conditions.

The *first* condition is obedience to the commandments of the Word. The *second* is to abide in Christ (John 15:7; 1 John 2:6). The *third* is to ask in Jesus' name (John 14:13, 14). This means far more than opening and closing our prayers with the expression, "In Jesus' name." It means to "put on" the Lord Jesus so we will look at things as He does. The *fourth* condition is "that the Father may be glorified in the Son" (John 14:13).

112

Who Is at the Hub?

God does not answer prayers that are to glorify self. Ask yourself this question: "Are you or is God the hub of your prayer life?" Prayers may be said in a wrong way or with a wrong motive. Some of the sharpest denunciations made by Jesus were directed at men who prayed. The scribes and the Pharisees were criticized for their motives, not for their praying. They were not condemned for praying in public, but for their insincerity.

Praying in self-will and for selfish desires may bring baneful consequences. Only God knows the end from the beginning. He knows what is best. For this reason we must bear in mind that the Word states: "If we ask any thing according to his will, he heareth us." God's will is found in His Word. When our prayers agree with His Word, He watches over our words and He answers. Believing prayer is linked to a life of living in Christ.

Is God Reluctant?

Prayer is not a means for us to persuade a reluctant God to do that which is against His better judgment. Prayer is coming to God for the fulfillment of His will. Praying in the will of God means our petitions will be in harmony with His holy and righteous character as revealed in His Word.

Often Christian young people have come to me soliciting my prayers for God's will about marriage. When conversation has revealed that the prospective mate is not a Christian, I have kindly but firmly stated that we need not pray for God's will in such a matter. He has stated His will in His Word—"Be ye not un-equally yoked together with unbelievers" (2 Corin-

113

thians 6:14). I will pray for that person's salvation, but not for their marriage. God has shown His will regarding the marriage of a believer to an unbeliever.

What's Your Motive?

Closely related to prayers that cannot be answered by God because they are not in His will, are those that are based on selfish motives. "Ye ask, and receive not, because ye ask amiss, that ye may consume it upon your lusts" (James 4:3). Nowhere does God bind himself to answer self-centered prayers. While He does promise to meet all our genuine needs, He does not agree to gratify our selfish desires. Ask yourself: "Is this prayer for God's glory, for my good, for the good of others, or simply to gratify my selfish desires?"

If

Another hindrance to answered prayer is a condemning heart. Sin may stand between us and God as a stumbling block to receiving an answer. The Psalmist declared, "If I regard iniquity in my heart, the Lord will not hear me" (Psalm 66:18). *The Speakers Bible* states: "The word 'regard' is happily chosen to express approval of iniquity." Jesus told the unbelieving Pharisees: "Now we know that God heareth not sinners: but if any man be a worshiper of God, and doeth his will, him he heareth" (John 9:31). And again John states:

> Beloved, if our heart condemn us not, then we have confidence toward God. And whatsoever we ask, we receive of him, because we keep his commandments, and do those things that are pleasing in his sight (1 John 3:21, 22).

114

Unforgiving, Miserly,
Dishonest, Inconsiderate

Other hindrances are an unforgiving spirit (Mark 11:25), a miserly spirit (Proverbs 21:13), and a dishonest life (Proverbs 28:9). Then there is the inconsiderate man whose prayers are hindered:

> Likewise, ye husbands, dwell with them according to knowledge, giving honor unto the wife, as unto the weaker vessel, and as being heirs together of the grace of life; that your prayers be not hindered (1 Peter 3:7).

When a husband and wife are ruled by selfishness in their relationship with each other, their prayer life becomes a casualty. What a need exists to build the family on loving mutuality and solid devotional life.

Do You Use the Key?

The final hindrance to be mentioned here is faithfulness. Faith is the indispensable key to the Christian life. Faith opens the earthly door to the measureless treasures of heaven. Faith opens the windows of heaven and brings to earth the power of God. Hebrews 11:6 states a basic principle of prayer: "Without faith it is impossible to please him: for he that cometh to God must believe that he is, and that he is a rewarder of them that diligently seek him."

We are to come to God in the confidence of faith, not in the deadness of despair. Maintain confidence; don't waver. James exhorts:

> Let him ask in faith, nothing wavering: for he that wavereth is like a wave of the sea driven with the wind and tossed. For let not that man think that he shall receive any thing of the Lord (James 1:6, 7).

A wave is here one second, gone the next. Don't believe one minute and doubt the next. Jesus said, "When you pray, believe," not, "When you believe, pray."

Worth Remembering

God is able—He can (Ephesians 3:20)!
God is willing—He will (Philippians 4:19)!
God is faithful—He does (Deuteronomy 7:9)!

Let faith dare to act (Genesis 12:1-4; 22:1-14; Hebrews 11:8). Let faith dare to trust God to act (Romans 4:13-23; Daniel 3:16, 17). Abraham and the three young Hebrews trusted totally. They knew God was *able, willing,* and *faithful.* Their doom seemed to be sealed, but they staggered not at the promise, and God answered. It was not faith in faith, but faith in God!

Learn to hear God's voice and to know His will. Love Him, His house, and His household. Be a good steward of your time, talents, and treasures. How do you do these things? They develop from your devotional life, your walk with God.

13

Pray One for Another

A British marine, Alexander Irvine, tells the story of a sea captain who used to pray in a salty way. The rugged commander loved to order sail drill in rough weather.

One day during a drill, the man out on the yardarm lost his grip and fell to the deck with a sickening thud. The next day the commander called the same drill, even though the weather was still bad. The new man also fumbled and fell to his death. The third day drill was ordered once again. The newly appointed foretop man was jovial Bill Hicks. He did not fall. He did his work and came down, laughing about it.

But there is an interesting sequel to this story. A few days later, when another ship drew near, an officer came on board and asked for Bill Hicks. He said to the captain: "We were 30 miles out to sea the other night when we saw a light flashing signals on the clouds. We told our signalman to take it down, and here is the message: 'God, this is Bill Hicks. I do not ask for no favors, just one. When I strike the foretops tomorrow, let me do it with the guts of a man. And, dear God, from this day forward give me the feelin' I used to have when I knelt at my mother's knee and said, "Our Father."'"

Bill Hicks was exactly himself before God. He

117

presented his problem; he knew that he needed God's help. When a person is at his wit's end, it is not a cowardly thing to pray; it is the only way to find assurance and peace. As long as we are self-sufficient and complacent, we think we don't need to ask God for anything. It is only when we know we are helpless and powerless that we reach out to God.

Do You "Use" God?

But, on the other hand, we must beware lest prayer becomes the seeking of a solution to personal problems rather than an act of worship and communion. Never "use" God as a means to selfish ends. There are far deeper dimensions to prayer than just "give me." Such dimensions in prayer are only learned by practice. A bride may receive a dozen cookbooks. But she won't learn to cook until she gets in the kitchen and does the job.

Jesus—Others—You

Devotional prayer ministry reaches beyond self to others. There are few things more liberating than a sincere concern for other people. Most of the prisons in which people find themselves are in part built by themselves.

If you really want spiritual liberty, pray for your friends. The person whose world centers on himself will always be a slave. The contract of personal liberty belongs to the person whose life is given to his friends. The termination of a lot of our problems comes when we break out of the prison of self to find liberation in earnest prayer for others. Make this order your practice: Jesus, Others, You—that's the way to spell JOY.

118

What About Job?

Too many of us find ourselves in the situation of Job. As long as he tried to clear himself of the blame that was heaped on him, he did not find deliverance. His three friends—Zophar, Eliphaz, and Bildad—spoke very harshly to him. They accused him of hypocrisy, thinking that all his actions were for the sake of gain, despite the fact that the Lord testified that he was a perfect and upright man (Job 1:8; 2:3). Perhaps nothing hurts more deeply than for an honest person to have his integrity questioned.

Job seemingly had every reason to become disgusted and completely disillusioned with his so-called friends. After the deep hurts he had suffered in the loss of his 10 children and all his possessions, plus his painful boils, condemning statements by proud and haughty men were uncalled for. Their verbal scourgings were premeditated. The Bible says, "They had made an appointment together." He seemed helpless, for his sickness kept him at their mercy.

But the Bible also says Job "prayed for his friends" (Job 42:10). To pray for them may have required great effort, but he did it. He stepped out of the realm of "I, me, and mine" into that of "we, us, ours, them, and theirs." After their cruel campaign, by a beautiful act of mind and heart, Job triumphed by praying for his friends.

What an answer to Job's prayer! "The Lord turned the captivity of Job." How Job must have thrilled! What a flow of adrenaline through every nerve and fiber of his tortured body! But more than that, "the Lord gave Job twice as much as he had before." Job 42:12 says: "So the Lord blessed the latter end of Job more than his beginning." He received twice as much as before of sheep, camels, oxen, and donkeys.

But Job had had seven sons and three daughters before his calamity. How come he didn't get 14 sons and 6 daughters? But he did — 10 of them had gone on before and now he had 10 more! And God gave Job 140 additional years to enjoy his "latter end"!

Praying for Those Who Harass You

The only time Jesus ever gave specific instructions concerning prayer for an unbeliever is recorded in Matthew 5:44 with its parallel passage in Luke 6:27, 28. These two passages are from the Sermon on the Mount and are instructions for us to pray for those who persecute us. This command is preceded by the command to love our enemies. We are to pray for those who "despitefully use" us. That term has the idea of insulting treatment and general harassment of a person.

Never will I forget the impact on my own thinking when a lady told me she was praying daily for Kruschev, the Soviet leader at the time. He was doing things that angered most Americans. A lot of people wished him dead. But here was a Christian who was burdened to pray for him.

How do you react to those who harass you? What about your boss? Your fellow workers on the job? The person who endeavors to make life miserable for you? Can you pray as Jesus did, "Father, forgive them" (Luke 23:34)?

Praying for One Another

The Bible commands us to pray for one another: "Pray one for another" (James 5:16). Even though it is a command with the added words: " . . . that ye may be healed," it is a command for us to pray for each other. Jesus said to Peter, "I have prayed for thee" (Luke 22:32). Our Lord prayed for Peter by name—for one individual. Paul prayed specifically for Timothy "night and day" (2 Timothy 1:3). He "always" prayed for Philemon (v. 4). Paul's prayers were largely intercessory prayers for others.

A partial list of those for whom Paul prayed, in addition to those mentioned above, includes: the Roman Christians, the Corinthians, the saints at Philippi, the Ephesians, the Colossians, and the Thessalonians. The apostle writes of Epaphras who always labored "fervently" in prayer for the Colossians (4:12). In turn, Paul requested of his friends, "Pray for me."

If I can't do anything to help my brother or sister in Christ with respect to some specific need he/she may have, I can at least pray for and with him/her. For this reason, I like to pause to pray with a friend whether it be in my office, in an airport, or even on the street.

Praying for All Saints

The Bible, by Paul's example, exhorts us to pray for all saints: "Praying always with all prayer and supplication in the Spirit, and watching thereunto with all perseverance and supplication for all saints" (Ephesians 6:18). If Christians would follow this exhortation, great blessing would result. Carping criticism would cease. Christian character would grow. Christ would be honored, and the body of Christ would profit.

The example of Paul in one of his prayers for the

Ephesians bears out his exhortation to pray for our fellow members in the body of Christ:

> For this cause I bow my knees unto the Father of our Lord Jesus Christ, of whom the whole family in heaven and earth is named, that he would grant you, according to the riches of his glory, to be strengthened with might by his Spirit in the inner man; that Christ may dwell in your hearts by faith; that ye, being rooted and grounded in love, may be able to comprehend with all saints what is the breadth, and length, and depth, and height; and to know the love of Christ, which passeth knowledge, that ye might be filled with all the fulness of God (Ephesians 3:14-19).

Praying for All Men

Prayer is to "be made for all men" (1 Timothy 2:1). This passage uses four of the strongest terms for prayer—"supplications, prayers, intercessions, and giving of thanks." Paul states that this is to be "first of all."

Praying for Your Rulers

Associated in the above exhortation to pray for all men is the specific instruction to pray "for kings, and for all that are in authority." God is vitally interested in earthly governments. From Romans 13:1 we learn that "the powers that be are ordained of God." For this reason we are to be subject to them (v. 5). The Lord counts on us to pray earnestly and intensely for all men and for all in authority that all people may hear the gospel and many of them may be saved (1 Timothy 2:1-4).

Praying for Your Pastor

Paul exhorts us to pray for God's ministers. On

more than one occasion, the apostle, as a minister, requested prayer for himself (1 Thessalonians 5:25; 2 Thessalonians 3:1, 2; Romans 15:30, 31; Philippians 1:19; Colossians 4:2-4).

You need to pray for your pastor:

1. That God will give him utterance and grace to preach all the counsel of God (2 Timothy 4:2; Colossians 4:2-4).

2. That God will fill his heart with love (1 Corinthians 13), faith (1 Timothy 1:12), and humility (2 Timothy 2:24-26).

3. That God may be glorified in all that he does (1 Peter 4:11; Philippians 1:19, 20).

4. That God will grant him the love and support of his parishioners (Romans 15:30-32).

Further, we ought to pray that God's minister will have:

1. A ministry patterned after Paul's words to the elders at Ephesus (Acts 20:17-36).

2. An ability to feed the flock (1 Peter 5:1-4).

3. A life and testimony void of offense (Hebrews 13:18; Acts 24:16; 1 Timothy 4:12).

4. A ministry of power in the Holy Spirit (1 Thessalonians 1:5; 2 Thessalonians 3:1).

5. A continuing unfolding of wisdom and revelation in the knowledge of Christ (Ephesians 1:15-23).

6. Deliverance from enemies (2 Corinthians 1:8-11; 2 Thessalonians 3:2).

7. The fulfillment of the ministry God gives him (Colossians 4:17; 2 Timothy 4:6-8).

Your pastor needs your encouragement and prayer. He does not need criticism and noncooperation. Pray for him as the servant of God.

Praying for Your Town

As Christians we are also encouraged to pray for the city in which we live (Jeremiah 29:7) and for Israel (Psalm 122:6).

Do You Care?

Let us never become so ingrown, friend, that we think God has everything now that He has us. We need to have concern for our neighbors and community. My street is to be my concern. Your street is your concern.

"It's the caring that counts." These words quoted by my pastor at a recent service gripped my attention. Jesus cares! If I am to be like Him, I must care! Jesus said of the Good Samaritan: "When he saw him, he had compassion on him, . . . and took care of him" (Luke 10:33, 34). People all around us are looking and longing for someone who cares.

A devotional life will develop a warm relationship with others. Communion with the Lord will deepen our love for God's people, enrich our family relationships, and make us better citizens. You cannot walk with God and fail to develop a spirit of sensitivity . . . caring.